T0246648

BRITAIN'S GHOSTS

'People think that ghosts only come out at night, or on Halloween, when the world is dark and the walls are thin. But the truth is, ghosts are everywhere.'

(Victoria Schwab, *City of Ghosts*, 2018)

BRITAIN'S GHOSTS

A SPINE-CHILLING TOUR OF OUR MOST HAUNTED PLACES

ANNA GROVES

National Trust

Published by National Trust Books
An imprint of HarperCollins Publishers
1 London Bridge Street, London SE1 9GF
www.harpercollins.co.uk

HarperCollins Publishers
Macken House, 39/40 Mayor Street
Upper, Dublin 1, D01 C9W8, Ireland

First published 2024
© National Trust Books 2024
Text © Anna Groves 2024
Illustrations © Augusta Akerman 2024

ISBN 978-0-00-866607-1

10 9 8 7 6 5 4 3 2

A catalogue record for this book is available from the British Library.

Printed and bound in the UK

If you would like to comment on any aspect of this book, please contact us at the
above address or national.trust@harpercollins.co.uk

National Trust publications are available at National Trust shops or online at
nationaltrustbooks.co.uk

This book is produced from independently certified FSC™ paper
to ensure responsible forest management.

For more information visit: www.harpercollins.co.uk/green

CONTENTS

INTRODUCTION

Welcome to *Britain's Ghosts*. This book will take you on a tour of the places that have played host to the ghostliest goings-on, that have borne witness to the most inexplicable events, and that have raised the hairs of those unfortunate enough to experience something for which they'll be consoled by few and disbelieved by many.

The 19th-century poet Henry Wadsworth Longfellow wrote:

> All houses wherein men have lived and died
> Are haunted houses. Through the open doors
> The harmless phantoms on their errands glide,
> With feet that make no sound upon the floors.

He wrote this about Chillingham Castle, which you can read about on page 117. Of course, it's not only the spirits of men that are believed to haunt our earthly realm. Between these covers you will find many a White Lady, several Tudor queens as well as the ghosts of children seeming to tarry between this world and the next.

On this paranormal tour of the UK we'll visit houses, hotels, palaces and pubs – the places where the dramas of human lives have played out, and which possess an uncanny sense of some of that drama continuing to play out, just out of sight, just beyond all our earthbound senses.

That's not to say that all the ghosts we'll encounter are housebound. We'll also be visiting as wide a variety of outdoor spaces – forests and gorges, moors and marshes, lakes and battlefields – where there is that same subliminal sense of something beyond the perception of our physical senses.

If all this sounds somewhat insubstantial, it's of course due to the subject matter. Many people are receptive to the idea of a place having a certain atmosphere, but relatively few have experienced something so unusual, so inexplicable that the events they relate become part of a myth, an unsolved mystery, something that defies explanation. If you're looking for answers, you won't find them here. If you're tirelessly curious and would like to think there's more beyond what we can see and feel in this world, there's intrigue in store.

Whether you're a believer in the existence of ghosts or not, you can't deny the existence of ghost stories, and there is not a part of the UK that doesn't have its stories to tell. Because ghosts are generally closely bound to a place, the stories told about them are often full of local history and all have their own distinct regional identity. So a tour of the country taking in each region's spookiest tales will really help us get under the skin of these places – and occasionally jump out of our own.

Indeed, it's arguable that these stories tell us more about the living than they do about the dead. The belief in ghosts, or at least the incomprehensible phenomena that can be experienced by the living when a person has died, has been around for as long as humans have been trying to make sense of death and what happens in the hereafter. In the mortal realm, fear of death is ever-present. It's something inescapable, but telling stories that arouse fear is one way developed by the ancients to help us at least briefly purge ourselves of it. Aristotle coined the term *catharsis* to describe this function performed by telling scary stories – Greek tragedy in his case.

So, the telling of scary stories can serve a function, one that has psychological benefits, and it's perhaps this continuing fascination with the *psychology* of the paranormal, rather than a widespread belief in the existence of the paranormal, that keeps ghosts alive in the popular imagination. In 2002, *Most Haunted* brought us the country's first paranormal reality television show (following complaints, Ofcom ruled it be classed as entertainment rather than investigative television) and has produced over 300 episodes to date. Some people watch it with an open mind, others are committedly sceptical, but everyone enjoys the suspense, the growing unease among the people in front of the camera, and secretly craves the moment they all scream and run out of the room in terror.

> There is an undeniable appetite for unsettling and other-worldly tales.

Most Haunted may have moved on to the internet but you can still find ghosts galore on television. In 2023, the BBC broadcast two documentaries – *Uncanny* and *Paranormal* – both of which invited contributions from psychologists and other members of the scientific community alongside opinion from experts in the paranormal. The BBC rounded off that year with the conclusion of one of its most successful sitcoms, *Ghosts*.

Indeed, the ghost story as a form of entertainment has existed down the centuries. From Pliny the Younger, in the 1st century AD, penning what some consider to be the earliest ghost story, through the golden era of Victorian ghost stories, to the slew of scary movies that come out in time for Halloween every year, it seems the ghost story is eternally fascinating to many. There is an undeniable appetite for unsettling and other-worldly tales, and stories that purport to be based on real events – or at least are made to look real (think of *The Blair Witch Project*) – are the most thrilling, even if they require more credulity than some can muster. It's possible to be sceptical, entertained and scared out of your wits all at the same time.

Many ghost stories require the backdrop of an often spooky, always old, house. And sometimes it works the other way round: in some circles, if a property is of a certain age, a resident ghost is considered a must-have. Some would go further and argue that the presence of ghosts is not just a marker of antiquity, but the unavoidable accumulation of spent lives. How can a building have seen so much history, so much of people's lives and not have an echo of at least some of those lives within its walls? Walls that could well have witnessed events so dramatic and traumatic that evidence, perhaps physical as well as metaphysical, is left after a person's passing.

So, it's an interest in our collective history, a curiosity about how people of the past lived their lives, an enduring, albeit morbid, fascination with what happens after we die – can this really be it? – that all come together in the form of ghost stories. We may not know what happens in the afterlife – if indeed anything happens at all – but it doesn't seem right to simply draw a veil over all those lives, and if we tell a few stories to help us connect with the people who have gone before, what really is the harm?

Whether you find these tales unsettling or remain unconvinced, it's hoped you'll at least be entertained. And like most stories, it's best not to make up your mind until you get to the end ....

SOUTH WEST

THE BUCKET OF BLOOD, CORNWALL

With such a name, this pub could be accused of false advertising if it didn't have tales to curdle the blood and chill the spine. It's a very Cornish curiosity that this county, now so desirable for its lush countryside and glorious coastline, was for so long besmirched by the grime of a world-leading mining industry and the violence of pirates, smugglers and wreckers. The Bucket of Blood – with its pretty 18th-century, Grade II-listed exterior – gives no clue as to its macabre moniker. The village of Phillack that it serves is equally picturesque, located less than a mile from Cornwall's Atlantic coast, separated by a range of sand dunes known as The Towans.

Being a village so close to the sea, Phillack's hostelry has drawn people who have business on the coast for centuries, whether that's building sandcastles, catching waves or smuggling contraband. With the oldest parts of the building dating from the late 13th century, it's doubtless gone by a few different names, so how did it come by this one?

Local legend goes that, one day, the landlord went out to draw water from the well. When he drew his bucket back up, it was filled with a viscous, crimson-coloured liquid. The well was investigated and the mutilated corpse of a customs officer was found, presumably dumped there when he got too close to uncovering some piratical racket. The place was literally infused with evil. Some say the unhappy spirit of the unfortunate official

lingers on, with sightings reported of a battered and bloodied man stumbling around outside the pub near the well.

That is the story most often told to explain the landlord's discovery of the tainted water. Another, far less interesting one, is that the water was polluted by run-off from the local tin mining industry. Again, mining and pirates – the grubbier side of Cornwall's history.

There have also been sightings besides that of the murder victim to suggest this pub is indeed haunted. While the ghost of the customs officer and the story of how he met his end give the pub its name, his is not the only resident spirit. Inside, a phantom monk has manifested in front of staff and patrons only to disappear again before their very eyes. He's been glimpsed mostly when staff are closing up for the night, or when they come to open up for the day. And between these hours, strange things have been going on, with staff on numerous occasions arriving in the morning to find tables and chairs rearranged and broken glass on the floor. Some people have even reported being grabbed or shoved by unseen hands.

If all that's a bit unsettling, it should be noted that the Bucket of Blood offers a customarily warm Cornish welcome and an excellent range of beers, ciders and spirits to calm the nerves. So, duly fortified, it's on to our next haunted property.

BUCKLAND ABBEY, DEVON

The tales of the oldest spirits still resident at Buckland Abbey originate from its time as a Cistercian monastery, founded in the 13th century. The monks who lived here all those centuries ago are seen on occasion, in the area of, but not quite on, the staircases. These structures were added after their time, so when the monks manifest they are seen to walk through the stairs cut off at the knee, as they tread the old abbey steps. The monks have a particularly strong presence in the Great Hall, as this was the heart of the abbey and where the nave would have been. The nave was used for the brothers' procession to the altar; just as they did then, they do in the afterlife. Monks are nothing if not devoted to their duties.

There have also been reports of two more presences in the Great Hall, dating to the abbey's more recent history. The first is the ghost of a man from the 1800s, who stays near the fireplace. It's thought this ghost belongs to a man named Charles, who died as the result of an accident while he was repairing the ceiling. The other presence is a woman, Catherine, who passed away a century earlier, but her demise was no accident. Her untimely undoing came at the hands of her husband, who drowned her in a nearby lake. Her ghost tends to closely follow after men, perhaps in hope of protection from her husband.

The kitchen would have been a busy room, with many people going about their tasks, and judging by the amount of paranormal activity reported here, so it remains. The fireplace seems to be a focal point of this activity, where sudden drops in temperature are often reported, as well as numerous sightings of spectral servants here. There is one maidservant in particular who, even in death, considers the kitchen still very much her domain. She has been seen walking purposefully around the fireplace, clearly focused on her never-ending work, and passing through the servants' door at the back of the room. Sometimes she also passes into the kitchen from the corridor outside and has been spotted from the doors in the Great Hall. So animated is she by her work, on occasion she has made her presence known by rocking the chair near the servants' door and by moving pots and pans around. With reports of doors slamming and presences passing between people in this room, the activity has been felt by some visitors to be so overwhelming that they've refused to enter.

These people might feel reassured by the fact that those who have seen or felt the presence of a ghost at Buckland Abbey have never reported feeling remotely threatened. These ghosts continue to linger either because there is business left undone or because their connection with the place is just so strong.

Another ghost who eternally tarries here is that of a well-dressed lady, who has been seen by many in several rooms of the house. Some who have seen her up close report a resemblance to Elizabeth Beatrice Drake, Lady Seaton, whose portrait hangs at Buckland Abbey. Whereas her ghost is seen in green, in her portrait she wears an ivory dress, the Drake Jewel hung about her neck, and stands in front of a tapestry depicting the defeat of the Spanish Armada associated with her famous forebear, Francis Drake. Lady Seaton was clearly extremely proud of her family history, and she devoted much energy to her ancestral home. In the 1920s she uncovered and restored the abbey's chapel. The excavations took place in what was the servants' hall

– perhaps this is what stirred the servants' ghosts from their spiritual repose? Lady Seaton's ghost has been known to appear in Drake's Chamber, particularly on rainy mornings, sometimes walking into the room or occasionally appearing beside people. She has also been spotted on the stairs next to the Georgian Dining Room and walking around on the top floor of the abbey. Hers is a far from menacing presence, sometimes accompanied by a sweet smell, with one report describing petals left in her wake that reappeared even after being vacuumed up.

Leaving Buckland's best till last, we come now to its most famous resident and ghost: Sir Francis Drake. Renowned seaman of the Elizabethan Age and one of the queen's favourites, Drake's great success brought him some detractors, who claimed he had signed a pact with the Devil. It was these supernatural powers that helped him defeat the Spanish Armada and, so the legend goes, rebuild Buckland Abbey in just three days. In 1596, during raids on Panama, Central America, Drake fell ill with dysentery. Shortly before he died, he ordered the drum that always accompanied him be taken back to Buckland and vowed that if England were ever in danger, someone should beat the drum and he would return to defend the country. Drake was buried at sea, but these words were preserved in another legend that says that the drum will be heard to beat at times of war. The last time it was heard was in 1939.

Drake's body may have slipped beneath the waves, but his soul (that some said he'd sold to the Devil) was condemned to ride for eternity in a coach pulled by headless horsemen across Dartmoor and followed by hellhounds. If any living dog hears one of these phantom hounds, they die instantly. It's to Dartmoor, the haunt of these devilish dogs, that we go next.

DARTMOOR, DEVON

The haunted historic house is a common enough concept, but there are many outdoor spaces that have equally long and rich traditions of human occupation, as well as an uncanny sense of past lives.

Perhaps it's the wildness of some outdoor spaces that causes people to see and experience the environment around them in more inquisitive ways. Who, or what, is out there? And, of course, the outdoors is where the elements play, sometimes rambunctiously, with the howling ferocity of the winds or the driving force of the rains. The landscape together with the weather, the light and the sounds of nature all conspire to give a spirit to a place: woods can confer a zen-like calm as you bathe in the dappled light of myriad shades of green; or they can arouse fear of what lurks in the undergrowth and tower intimidatingly over you with their bare skeletal branches.

Dartmoor is a wild-looking place – even on the stillest of days the trees are tortuously bent in the direction of the prevailing wind – and it's full of dramatic backdrops: rivers that thunder through gorges, woods that whisper in the breeze, bogs that can engulf the unwary and tors that keep their stony vigil over the moor's comings and goings. And drama it has most certainly seen, with some events easily relayed and understood, but others defying rational explanation.

One haunting piece of Dartmoor folklore arguably inspired Sir Arthur Conan Doyle's most famous tale, *The Hound of the Baskervilles*. The author is reputed to have based his story of a hellish hound with glowing eyes on local reports of such a beast, which for generations has stalked the moor. While the ever-rational and scientific Sherlock Holmes debunked the tale – revealing that a villainous nephew, who felt deprived of his inheritance, had starved and mistreated a large dog, covering it in phosphorus to make it glow in the dark – the origins of the story Doyle adapted are far more mysterious.

The local legend was reported in the *Daily Express* and read by Doyle, who was moved to investigate further. In June 1901, Doyle explored Dartmoor in the company of the reporting journalist, Bertram Fletcher Robinson. Doyle learned of Richard Cabell, a 17th-century squire, also known as 'Dirty Dick', who had acquired the moniker for several dastardly deeds, including the murder of his wife. Described by contemporaries as a 'monstrously evil man', he is said to have lived only for hunting and had sold his soul to the Devil. His love of hunting and this diabolical pact gave rise to the tradition: the night he died and was laid to rest, a pack of phantom hounds came prowling and howling around his tomb. When the hounds weren't at Cabell's graveside, they were out terrorising locals and their animals. In order to contain his soul, the villagers laid a large slab over the tomb and built a mausoleum around it for good measure. It appears to have worked; you can visit the Cabell Mausoleum in the graveyard of Holy Trinity Church in Buckfastleigh without fear of being bothered by hellhounds.

LYDFORD GORGE, DEVON

On the western edge of Dartmoor you'll find Lydford Gorge, the deepest river gorge in the South West and one that stretches for a mile and a half. The descent into the gorge can be challenging in places, but it's worth the effort as you venture further and deeper into a landscape that is all at once ancient, mysterious and elemental.

The River Lyd wends its way through millennia-old, moss-covered, slate-grey rocks – in some places flowing serenely, in others swirling thunderously. On the steep slopes either side, woodland roots itself precariously in the shallow soil, occasionally crowding out the sunlight, stilling the damp air, creating an other-worldly atmosphere, far removed from modern life.

If pixies were going to live anywhere, this is where they'd be. Pixies pop up in British folklore from across the regions, but they seem to be particularly concentrated in Devon and Cornwall. Though human in form, pixies are elemental creatures, closely bound to nature, who spend most of their time dancing, wrestling and riding Dartmoor ponies. When they do interact with humans, it's often to point out misdeeds or to reward considerate behaviour. Dartmoor pixies are thought to be helpful, particularly with the housework, provided their work is rewarded. But cross a pixie and that's when they'll unleash all their mischievous tricks. There are perils and pitfalls enough walking in Lydford Gorge without offending a pixie, so here they are welcomed and respected, and they have their very own designated area at Pixie Glen.

At the other end of the gorge from Pixie Glen, after the many dramatic twists and turns and changes of scenery that you'll experience at Lydford Gorge, you come to Whitelady Waterfall. She is a spectacular cascade, the tallest in the South West at almost 30 metres, and people have been coming to admire her long flowing form for centuries, although some have seen more than they bargained for.

Stories tell of a spectre dressed in a long white gown who haunts the base of the waterfall. Some say that anyone drowning in the river will be saved by her, whereas others believe that seeing her is a sign that you are about to meet your end. A 19th-century writer, John Lloyd Warden Page, urged caution; perhaps it was safer to 'keep clear of her embrace' than to test the theory (*The Rivers of Devon*, 1893).

Sometimes confused with the White Lady, but in fact connected to events that took place at the opposite end of the gorge, is the ghost of a woman who haunts Kitts Steps. The earliest reference dates to 1804, when a story was related of an unfortunate woman who found the gushing river in full flow on her way back from market. Unwisely, she decided to attempt the crossing on her pony and both were washed away. A later version, from 1833, adds a few more details in that she was called Catherine or 'Kitty' and she was returning from Okehampton market. The same misjudgement led to her sad demise, but this time the pony survived and was later found grazing on a nearby bank. Half a happy ending.

CHAMBERCOMBE MANOR, DEVON

This manor house could hardly look any more inviting, with its white-washed stone walls, neatly lidded dormer windows and informal, cottage-garden-style planting. First recorded in the Domesday Book of 1086, for nearly a millennium it has stood in its wooded valley, or combe, a picture of bucolic tranquillity. But a lot can happen in a thousand years and the fortunes of this house, and its occupants, have waxed and waned greatly over time.

In the 12th century, Chambercombe was the residence of Sir Henry Champernon, Lord of the Manor of Ilfracombe, and it remained the property of that family for many generations. In 1530 it became the country seat of Henry Grey, Duke of Suffolk and father of Lady Jane Grey. Father and daughter both lost their heads, Jane after serving as the Nine Days' Queen and her father after getting caught trying to overthrow the new queen, Mary. Three hundred years later, a mummified head was found in the vault of a church close to the Tower of London and identified by a local antiquarian as that of Henry, hidden by his widow to prevent it being displayed on a spike. Although this sounds the perfect set-up, there is unfortunately no tale of a headless man haunting Chambercombe, though visitors to the manor have reported many other sightings.

One of the ghosts believed to haunt Chambercombe Manor is the spirit of a young woman who lived and died here in the 17th century, but whose earthly remains weren't discovered until

1738. The owner at that time, Jan Vye, was carrying out some renovations and noticed a void between walls with no access. He might have thought this was a happy discovery – he could have that en suite after all – but what he uncovered was the skeletal remains of a woman, still dressed and laid out on a bed draped with fabric. What follows is the tragic tale of how this unfortunate woman was denied a properly observed burial and came instead to be incarcerated in this gruesome garret.

Perhaps due to the ignominy of Henry Grey's treasonous behaviour and subsequent beheading, Chambercombe Manor lost its status as a seat of nobility. A series of tenants and owners who lived here worked for their living, some of them honestly, such as the farmers who toiled and tilled the land or tended flocks and herds, and some of them dishonestly, such as the wreckers who preyed on vessels that floundered on the rocks of the North Devon coast. These land-lubbing brigands would venture out on particularly dark and stormy nights in hope of spotting a ship in distress. They would then turn on their lanterns, hoping the crew would mistake the shining lights for helpful beacons and be lured onto the rocks, so the ship could then be plundered. There are reports of survivors of shipwrecks even being murdered for the possessions they were washed ashore with.

One visitor reported that she began to cry uncontrollably as she approached what she called the secret room.

Alexander Oatway was one such wrecker who was living at Chambercombe Manor in the 17th century. He had a son, William, who as a young man did not have the stomach for the family business and even rescued a Spanish woman from a wreck and married her. They had a daughter, Kate, who grew up and fell in love with an Irish naval officer, Duncan Wallace, whom she married and went to live with in Dublin, promising to one day make a return visit.

Meanwhile, William had inherited not only Chambercombe Manor but also his father's gambling debts, forcing him to rethink his views on wrecking as a means of keeping a roof over his and his wife's head. One night in 1695, William went out with his wrecking crew to see what they could pick off a stricken ship. He found a woman, barely alive and badly disfigured from being repeatedly tossed against the rocks. He took her home, presumably in the hope that he and his wife might save her, but the woman's injuries were too great. Having failed in his

altruistic bid to save another's life, his piratical urges took over and he helped himself to the jewels the women was wearing.

One story goes that William overheard sailors who had survived the wreck talking in a tavern about their dead captain, Captain Wallace; another that a shipping agent was making enquiries in the area about a missing passenger, Mrs Kate Wallace. When William realised what he had done – stolen from the lifeless body of his own daughter – he boarded up the room in which his daughter lay, and left Chambercombe for good. It's said that his wife died shortly after this tragic event.

While this overwhelmingly sad tale has left its mark on the place – one visitor in 2010 reported that she began to cry uncontrollably as she approached what she called the secret room and that she felt utter despair, loss and sadness – Chambercombe Manor is not a sad place. Visitors agree and so do some of the other ghosts. The spirits of two little girls continue to play here, and those who have sensed their presence have described them as happy and clearly enjoying themselves; although perhaps a bit too much, as they are prone to a spot of teasing and have been known to try to catch people's attention by moving things around.

And then there have been other peculiar goings-on when the whole house has been felt by some to move. Numerous visitors have reported their legs going weak, or have felt queasy and unsteady. This frequently observed phenomenon is believed to be due to the timbers in some parts of the house having had former lives at sea, recycled from ocean-going and storm-tossed ships. As soon as those affected in this way leave the property, they feel perfectly normal again, leaving several self-professed sceptics unable to explain what came over them.

GLASTONBURY TOR, SOMERSET

'The green isle of Glaston, severed as it was from the outer world by its girdle of marsh and mere, was from old time a haunt of peace.' So begins Frederick Bligh Bond's book *The Gates of Remembrance*. Generally known as Bligh, he was an architect, archaeologist and, somewhat more curiously, a psychical researcher. He came to Glastonbury in 1908, when he was appointed director of excavations at Glastonbury Abbey by the Church of England. His book, published a decade later, detailed his psychical research methods and revealed that his excavations had been guided by the spirits of long-dead monks, who communicated with him through his friend, the medium John Alleyne. His ecclesiastical employers promptly sacked him.

Bligh would not have been the first, and was certainly not the last, to be struck by the veil of mysticism that Glastonbury wears. It's a place that has been shrouded in mystery and myth for millennia. There is a tradition that St Joseph of Arimathea came here in the early days of Christianity to preach and brought with him the Holy Grail, which he buried just below Glastonbury Tor. In that spot, you'll find the Chalice Well. In Celtic mythology the tor went by the name *Ynys Witrin* ('Isle of Glass') and was believed to be the entrance to the underworld and home to Gwyn ap Nudd, the Lord of the Otherworld. And then, perhaps most famously, there is Glastonbury's connection to King Arthur, who is said to have been buried beneath the abbey. In the 12th century, the monks of the abbey apparently discovered two skeletons – one of a man and one of a woman, whose golden hair was still attached – which were assumed to have once been Arthur and Guinevere. It was presumably these monks who were feeding the information to Bligh.

So the veil between this realm and whatever lies beyond has long been regarded as gossamer thin at Glastonbury. For some, Glastonbury is the occult capital of England. Many people have reported seeing ghosts in the town, whether they came looking for them or not. Some of these have been visitors staying at the George and Pilgrims Hotel, built in the 15th century to accommodate visitors to the nearby abbey, and now considered to be one of the most haunted hotels in the country.

One of the most regular sightings is of a monk who drifts down the corridors and an elegant woman wearing a look of longing who sometimes follows him, but always at a distance. A medium who came to investigate believes they are two would-be lovers, the monk's apparent choice of the Church over his beloved leaving the pair to pine for eternity.

Another ghost that takes the form of a portly monk cuts a more cheerful figure, even as he disappears through walls. He apparently chuckles as he goes and the people who have seen him report feelings of happiness and delight.

Considering herself less fortunate, perhaps, was the wife of a travel journalist, staying at the George and Pilgrims for an assignment. She woke in the night to see a tall man with long arms looking at her from the foot of the bed. Deciding she needed to reach out to touch him to prove what she was seeing, her hand passed right through, her subsequent screams waking her husband. She certainly discovered, like so many others, that there is so much more to Glastonbury than meets the eye.

THE ANCIENT RAM INN, GLOUCESTERSHIRE

We started our tour of some of the South West's most haunted places with a stiffener in The Bucket of Blood. Our last stop in the region no longer operates as a pub, as it did for much of its 800-year-plus history, but is now run as a tourist attraction specialising in paranormal experiences.

The Ancient Ram Inn is the oldest building in the historic town of Wotton-under-Edge on the southern fringe of the Cotswolds. It's thought to have been built in the 12th century as

a lodge for the labourers constructing St Mary's Church a short distance away, and then served as a priest's house before being converted to a pub.

It's seen such history, so much of human life, and death, that its claim to be the most haunted building in Britain is unsurprising. Then when you consider the inn is built on the intersection of two ley lines – paths of energy connecting sites of spiritual significance, with one of these paths connecting the inn with Glastonbury – it supports the idea that something out of the ordinary might be going on here. And when you learn that the inn also occupies the site of an ancient pagan burial ground, it would be surprising if this place *wasn't* buzzing with paranormal activity.

When The Ancient Ram Inn ceased to serve as a pub in 1968, it was bought by a man named John Humphries, who was intent on saving the ancient building from ruin. It seems to have tried to resist his attentions however and, according to Humphries, on his first night at the property he was dragged from his bed by demonic forces. Many wouldn't have stayed a minute longer but he persevered and, despite frequent disturbing episodes and discoveries, he made the building's preservation his life's work.

> *It's seen such history that its claim to be the most haunted building in Britain is unsurprising.*

For a time, the inn was run as a guesthouse, but gradually its reputation put off all but the most fearlessly curious. You can still stay here, though it's for those in pursuit of the paranormal rather than a comfortable night's sleep followed by a cooked breakfast and a stroll in the Cotswolds.

It's said there are up to 20 resident ghosts but some are better known than others. There's a 15th-century woman who was sentenced to death for witchcraft. She tried to take refuge in the building but was dragged away and burned at the stake. In the walls of the room now called the Witch's Room, Humphries discovered a mummified cat, which had seemingly been placed there to ward off evil spirits (see also page 135, Newton House).

Other discoveries made during Humphries' renovation included several children's skeletons, with broken knives still inside. The sound of children crying has been reported throughout the inn, echoing down the millennia since the site was in use as a pagan burial ground where human sacrifices were believed to have taken place.

In the most haunted room, the Bishop's Room, there are reputed to be no fewer than nine spirits, including a dark monk, some bishops and nuns, but also the spirit of a small cavalier King Charles spaniel. The ghost of a young woman has been seen hanging by her legs from the ceiling. The screams of a man who was murdered in this room by having his head thrust into the fireplace have also been heard. And a Roman centurion on horseback has manifested and passed straight through the wall, terrifying two plumbers in the process (see also page 106, Treasurer's House). In the attic it's said that an innkeeper's daughter was murdered, and people attempting to sleep in the Bishop's Room below – where incidentally the bed has been known to levitate – have heard 'something heavy' being dragged across the floor above.

It's easy to see why Humphries struggled to run the place as a bed and breakfast, but the final straw was apparently the incubus (a demon in male form that tries to have sex with sleeping women) in one of the rooms. The same room had a succubus, the female equivalent, but there were no complaints of molestation from male guests.

No room at the inn is safe. In the kitchen, Humphries was thrown against the wall by an unseen force, something that also happened to a young man years later during a ghost hunt. Two people ran from this room when they saw an apparition of a young woman rise up through the floor. The bodies of a woman and her baby were later found in that spot. Another young woman was found buried under the bar, which is next to the kitchen. She appeared to Humphries' daughter on multiple occasions and introduced herself as Elizabeth, saying she'd been murdered by a highwayman. There is a space in the roof that was known to be used as a highwaymen's hiding place.

With so many ghosts under one roof, The Ancient Ram Inn has good claim to be the most haunted building in Britain, but there are many more places to be explored, so on we go eastwards into London for our next destination.

GREATER LONDON AND SOUTH EAST

SUTTON HOUSE, LONDON

Sutton House is Hackney's oldest surviving example of a residential building. It was built in 1535 by Sir Ralph Sadleir, one of Henry VIII's Privy Councillors who in 1540 ascended to the position of Secretary of State. As a statesman's residence it features fine oak-panelled rooms, a grand staircase, a great hall and ornately carved fireplaces, which have survived the ages and the various uses of the house – including a trade union office from the 1950s and a squat where a range of community activities took place in the 1980s. It was subsequently taken in hand by the National Trust and restored, with artefacts from every period of occupation preserved.

The restoration uncovered more than the building's physical layers of history. An architectural student who was living in the house in the early 1990s woke one night to find a lady, dressed in blue, hovering over his bed. Years later, a National Trust house steward encountered the same spectre while sleeping in the same room, but she apparently announced her presence far more insistently, by violently shaking his bed.

Curiosity aroused, a seance was held at the house by local spiritualists who detected the presence of several spirits in residence, naming two of them as Tim and George. This was at a time when Sutton House was the subject of much interest and research, being a house of great antiquity, recently restored and reopened to the public. Shortly before the seance, but before he'd had a chance to report any of his findings, a local historian had been examining records relating to the house and discovered that after it was divided into two in 1751, the two tenants were listed as Timothy Ravenhill and George Garrett.

The spiritualists also detected ill-feeling between the pair, despite both being silk weavers and both being of Huguenot descent, and their bickering seems to have carried on into the afterlife. The poltergeist-type activity reported at the house – sudden drops in temperature, objects flung across rooms – could be manifestations of this eternal ill will.

Spiritualists are not the only ones who've picked up discomforting vibrations at Sutton House – visiting assistance dogs have been known to freeze in their tracks in certain rooms. This could be to do with the bickering neighbours, or the dogs, sometimes heard, but never seen, at night. One of Sutton

House's owners in the 16th century, a wool merchant called John Machell, is known to have had three dogs, described variously as lurchers and wolfhounds. A housekeeper employed by the National Trust reported that when she locked up every night, she felt wiry hair brushing against her right hand.

The final phantom to mention at Sutton House is the White Lady (as it would be unusual for a house of this great age to be without one). John Machell's daughter-in-law, Frances, died while giving birth to twins in the house and it's thought the White Lady is her ghost in mourning. The first report was made by a union official who saw such an apparition glide past an open door, but when she stepped out to investigate, the figure in white had vanished. Then, in the 1980s, a photo was taken outside the community centre's café bar of a group of friends – plus one not physically present at the party. She was dressed in white and held her arms outstretched, perhaps pleading to be reunited with her babies.

TOWER OF LONDON

Despite its reputation as primarily a place of detention and execution, the Tower of London has performed many other functions over its nearly 1,000-year history – an armoury, a treasury, a menagerie, a mint. Its official title is His Majesty's Royal Palace and Fortress of the Tower of London and it occupies an area of almost 12 acres bounded by castle walls. At its centre is a keep called the White Tower, which gives the entire complex of buildings its name.

From its foundation shortly after the Norman Conquest of 1066, the Tower of London was built to visually dominate and exude power and control over Saxon London. From the outset, the tower was fearfully regarded as a symbol of oppression. But it was during the Tudor period that it gained its enduring reputation as a grim and forbidding prison, where the treasonous were left to rot and the even less fortunate lost their heads. This reputation would have served the monarchy well, acting as a warning to any would-be traitors, but the truth is that only 10 people were executed within the walls of the Tower of London, three queens among them.

The first of those select but unfortunate few was William Hastings, 1st Baron Hastings, in 1483 and six more nobles were executed during the reigns of Henry VIII and his daughter Elizabeth I. Over a century later, three commoners joined that august line-up: three soldiers of the Black Watch Scottish infantry regiment who met their ends before a firing squad for desertion in 1743 (see page 78, Lyveden).

It was the quality rather than the quantity of executions that sent shockwaves down through history, as they were intended to, and gave rise to the tower's most famous ghost, Anne Boleyn. The second wife of Henry VIII was beheaded on 19 May 1536 and her headless ghost has been seen close to the site as well as leading a procession in the chapel. In 1864, Captain J.D. Dundas of the Yeoman Warders, also known as Beefeaters, saw one of his men attempting to charge a 'whitish, female figure' with his bayonet in the courtyard where Anne was beheaded. Rather than running her through, the man ran through her, to his great surprise. Manifesting and dematerialising are what ghosts are known to do, and time and place are no barriers to them: Anne is said to also haunt her family home at Blickling in Norfolk (see page 85).

While Anne's end was brutal, it was mercifully swift, as she was the only person to be executed in the tower by sword rather than axe. Consider poor Margaret Pole, Countess of Salisbury, whose crime was to be the mother of Cardinal Pole, a critic of Henry VIII's decision to appoint himself head of the Church of England. An eyewitness to her execution in 1541 described how a 67-year-old woman was made to kneel before a 'wretched and blundering youth' who failed to strike her neck and hacked instead at her head and shoulders. A woman's screams have been caught in the air by visitors to the site, a chilling echo of that grisly fate.

Two more ghosts, taking the heartbreaking shape of two terrified boys, join the spectral ranks at the tower. They are thought to be 12-year-old Edward V and his younger brother Richard, who were sent by their uncle, the Duke of Gloucester, to the tower for their own safety after Edward succeeded to the throne. The boys were never seen again, and their uncle claimed the throne as Richard III. In 1674, two small skeletons were discovered by workmen and many historians argue these are the remains of the unfortunate boys, murdered by their uncle. The ghosts of two boys have been seen on many occasions, dressed in their nightgowns, clutching each other in terror.

Another suspected murder victim whose spirit's bound to the tower is Arbella Stuart. She was a distant cousin of Elizabeth I and her crime was to marry William Seymour –also distantly related to a former queen, Lady Jane Grey – without royal consent. Seeing this as a move on her part to position herself as a contender for the Crown, King James placed Arbella under arrest in the tower. He didn't get the chance to have her executed, however, as she starved to death, either by the cruelty of her captors or by her own refusal to eat.

As well as the place where high-profile prisoners were detained, sometimes to the death, the tower was a scene of torture, where practitioners skilled in nearly killing people plied their trade. One of the most famous victims was Guy Fawkes, who was brought to the tower to be interrogated in November 1605. A member of the group of conspirators who hatched a plot to assassinate James I by blowing up the Houses of Parliament during its State Opening, Fawkes was tortured to give up the names of his co-conspirators. Once he'd confessed, Fawkes and three others were dragged behind a horse to Westminster's Old Palace Yard, where they were hanged, drawn and quartered. James I personally instructed the torturers: 'If he will not other ways confesse, the gentler tortures are first to be used upon him, and then step by step you may employ the harsher, and so speede youre goode work.' What the 'gentler tortures' could have been is not known, but it's likely Fawkes was put on the rack, a device designed to slowly pull the body limb from limb. Fawkes's agonised cries are believed to reverberate in the dungeons still.

It wasn't only humans who suffered torture and death at the tower. In the Middle Ages, monarchs were in the habit of gifting each other animals. In 1235 the Holy Roman Emperor Frederick II gave three big cats (described as leopards but probably lions) to Henry III, inspiring him to start a menagerie at the tower. In 1252 he received a polar bear, thought to be a gift from the King of Norway, and in 1255 the King of France sent an elephant. By 1622 the menagerie included three eagles, two pumas, a tiger and a jackal, as well as more big cats, which were the most popular attractions. Sadly, also popular in 16th- and 17th-century London was bear-baiting. Mercifully, this practice was permanently outlawed by an Act of Parliament in 1835, the same year in which the menagerie was closed. The animals were sent to a new home in Regent's Park but some, it appears, stayed on. The ghost of a bear is said to appear from behind a door in the Jewel House and, more curiously still, in 1816 a similar sighting was reported near the Martin Tower, where the Crown Jewels were kept until the 1840s when the collection was moved to purpose-built accommodation.

Today the only animals kept captive at the Tower of London are the famous ravens, and you can be sure they are very well looked after – the continued existence of the monarchy and the country depend on it!

CANTERBURY CATHEDRAL, KENT

Canterbury has evidence of human occupation dating to the Stone Age. The Cantiaci, an Iron Age people, made it their main settlement, which the Romans captured in the 1st century AD, building a city on the site. When the Romans left these shores in 410, it remained abandoned until the Jutes arrived from mainland Europe and made it the capital of the Kingdom of Kent. In 597, Saint Augustine was sent by Pope Gregory to Christianise the Anglo-Saxons and founded Canterbury

Cathedral. In the 11th century the cathedral was entirely rebuilt as the glorious edifice you see today, which would have been draw enough, but it was the murder of Archbishop Thomas Becket inside the cathedral in 1170 that made it a famous place of pilgrimage.

A place of such antiquity with a high-profile murder to boot could be expected to be chock-full of phantoms, and that it is, but not the ones you might expect. Canterbury Cathedral's primary ghost is not that of Thomas Becket but of another murdered archbishop, Simon of Sudbury. He was killed by Wat Tyler, the leader of the Peasants' Revolt, at our last stop, the Tower of London – which proved to be the archbishop's last stop too.

Simon was appointed archbishop in 1375 and Lord Chancellor in 1380, at a time when the country's treasury had been badly depleted by the Hundred Years' War with France. The conflict had been going since 1337, so that's not what they called it at the time, but the king and his chancellor clearly knew there were many more years of war to come, so Simon was tasked with taxing the nation to raise funds. This would prove to be his undoing. On 14 June 1381, Simon was taken by an angry mob of revolting peasants from the Tower of London and beheaded just outside the walls on Tower Hill. He was not well executed and apparently it took eight clumsy strokes of an axe for his head to be severed from his body. His head was placed on a spike above the gatehouse on London Bridge, the usual treatment of a traitor, only to be joined there the very next day by Wat Tyler's head.

The revolt quashed, Archbishop Simon's body was taken to Canterbury Cathedral and laid to rest with full ceremony but with a cannonball in place of a head. His head was taken down from London Bridge after six days by William Walworth, the Lord Mayor of London, and was taken to St Gregory's Church in Sudbury, Suffolk, where it's still displayed today. Being in literally two places at the same time, Simon's ghost is said to haunt both St Gregory's and Canterbury Cathedral. What's more, in Sudbury it's his disembodied footsteps that are heard – whereas his feet are in Canterbury – and in Canterbury he is recognised by his face, which is in a display case in Sudbury.

Also said to haunt the cathedral is the ghost of Nell Cook, a canon's servant who discovered that her employer was having an affair, some say with his niece. Nell took their punishment into her own hands and poisoned them with pie. When her crime was uncovered, she was buried alive beneath a passage in the cathedral known as the Dark Entry. Her horrific ordeal was put into rhyming couplets by R.H. Barham in *The Ingoldsby Legends* (1837): 'But I've been told that moan and groan, and fearful wail and shriek / Came from beneath that paving-stone for nearly half a week – / For three long days and three long nights came forth those sounds of fear; / Then all was o'er – they never more fell on the listening ear.'

Or did they? It's said that Nell still silently haunts the passage and still she threatens death to those unfortunate enough to encounter her: 'But one thing's clear – that all the year on every Friday night, / Throughout that Entry dark doth roam Nell Cook's unquiet Sprite ... / And whoso in that Entry dark doth feel that fatal breath, / He ever dies within the year, some dire, untimely death.'

PRESTON MANOR, EAST SUSSEX

Preston Manor, just outside Brighton, has been much altered over the centuries, though parts of the original 13th-century building survive internally. Today it's run as a museum dedicated to the Edwardian era. While it displays the comfort and elegance of that period, Preston Manor also has a reputation as one of the most haunted houses in Britain. Documented sightings of a variety of phantoms date back to the 16th century, and a manifestation of the manor's most famous ghost in the late 1800s drew particular attention.

Twin girls, Lily and Diana Macdonald, were born at Preston Manor in 1866 and both were familiar with the White Lady, whom they'd seen during their childhood. Lily never married and was still living at Preston Manor at the end of 1896, when she again encountered the White Lady. She was moved to give an account of it to the house's first curator, Henry Roberts. In his words: 'Miss Lily Macdonald tells me that in October or November 1896 as she was trying a new lampshade in the Drawing Room at Preston Manor, the ghost walked in at the door and came straight to her as if to speak. Miss M recognised it as the ghost, seeing her white dress and hair hanging down. She followed the ghost through the Billiard Room to the foot of the stairs, then put her arm around her saying "No – you don't go now". Miss M's arms went through the figure and it disappeared at once.'

The White Lady appears to have been active that winter, as a guest at the manor reported seeing her in the entrance hall. A seance was organised soon after, during which it was revealed that she was the spirit of an excommunicated nun, Sister Agnes, who'd been buried in unconsecrated land. The very next year, in 1897, the remains of a middle-aged woman were found behind the house during drainage works. The owners of Preston Manor arranged for the body to be interred in St Peter's churchyard in the grounds of the manor and sightings were fewer, but didn't stop altogether.

In 1903, Lily and Diana's mother, Eleanor, was on her deathbed in the Blue Bedroom, her night nurse keeping vigil. The White Lady made a final appearance to Eleanor just before she died, scaring poor Nurse Glasspool witless in the process. Not that there's any mention of the White Lady as a sinister presence, with more evidence suggesting she is a benign entity. Eleanor's grandson John Bennet-Stanford wrote in 1935: 'She is quite harmless and interesting … was a great friend of my grandmother, Mrs Macdonald, who constantly saw her.'

Less benign are the two phantom men another of Eleanor's daughters saw fighting on a staircase. She also described an 'immensely evil' presence in a nearby bedroom, where two visitors on separate occasions reported seeing the same thing: a disembodied hand moving up and down the four-poster bed. Activity associated with a poltergeist has also been reported on this side of the house – objects being moved around, holes being cut into dresses, and doors opening and closing of their own accord – but the organisers of the ghost tours held regularly at the manor are confident there is no danger posed, so you're free to find out for yourself.

HAMPTON COURT PALACE, LONDON

Hampton Court Palace is world-famous as the favourite residence of Henry VIII, a man whose favour was unreliably conferred. It was in fact built by his chief minister, Cardinal Thomas Wolsey, but as Wolsey fell from the king's favour when he failed to persuade the pope to annul Henry's first marriage, he felt obliged to give the palace to Henry to stay on his good side. Because we all know what happened to those of whom Henry tired. Being married to Henry VIII had a rather low survival rate of 50 per cent: Anne Boleyn and Catherine Howard were executed, and Jane Seymour died from postpartum complications.

Henry's second wife, Anne Boleyn, enjoyed the comfort and splendour of Hampton Court Palace for some of the three years she was married to the king. When her time was up, she was taken away to the Tower of London where she was beheaded. Anne's ghost is surely the most well-travelled of Britain's ghosts, using the ethereal superhighway to manifest in multiple locations (see page 34, Tower of London and page 85, Blickling Hall). At Hampton Court, she appears dressed in blue or black and walks the corridors in disconsolate fashion, with her head in her hands, literally.

The king's third wife, Jane Seymour, had the 'blessing' of dying of natural causes. She also had the honour of being the only one of Henry's wives to be interred alongside him in the royal tomb at Windsor Castle (although her heart and other organs were buried somewhere underneath the high altar in the Chapel Royal at Hampton Court). This privilege was because she produced the male heir for which Henry so longed, Prince Edward. But the poor woman died just days after giving birth. She is a seldom-seen spectre, who revisits Hampton Court on the anniversary of Edward's birth, 12 October 1537, and lingers on the Silverstick Stairs carrying a lighted taper, a lost soul looking for her lost baby. Truly, this is where her heart resides.

The fifth wife, Catherine Howard, was, like Anne before her, accused of adultery and treason, and was beheaded. She was queen for just over a year and only 19 when she was accused and arrested. The fate of her predeceased predecessor must have been known to her and the girl was surely terrified. It's said that when the guards came to take her away, she ran screaming down a corridor – now called the Haunted Gallery – begging for mercy. This is the awful moment that is the tape loop of her trapped and tormented soul. The way she haunts Hampton Court makes her unmissable and has led to her being somewhat unsympathetically nicknamed 'The Screaming Queen'. Even when her presence is not seen or heard, Catherine's ghost seemingly has the power to affect – visitors often report feelings of coldness and dizziness, with two women on separate tours reportedly fainting on the exact same spot in the Haunted Gallery.

It's not only queens who haunt Hampton Court, as a royal servant is said to be still in residence. Sybil Penn was Prince Edward's wetnurse and looked after Elizabeth, Henry's daughter with Anne. When Elizabeth contracted smallpox as a young woman in 1562, Sybil nursed her throughout. Elizabeth recovered but Sybil contracted the illness, died and was buried at

St Mary's Hampton in Middlesex. Sybil appears to have had centuries of spiritual repose, but when the church was rebuilt in 1829 and her tomb was disturbed, there were frequent reports at Hampton Court of a grey wraith in female form. One of the people to see her was Princess Frederica of Hanover, who described 'a tall, gaunt figure, dressed in a long grey robe, with a hood on her head and her lanky hands outstretched before her'.

One of Princess Frederica's guards also claimed to have seen a woman in a grey hooded robe in a room on the first floor who vanished before his eyes. Around the same time, and in the same room, strange noises resembling the sound of a spinning wheel were reported coming from a wall. When investigated, a sealed chamber was found and inside was – you've guessed it already – an old spinning wheel.

HINTON AMPNER, HAMPSHIRE

We've heard many stories of houses with ghosts. This is a story about a ghost of a house, one that was so bedevilled by ghosts it had to be demolished. The old Tudor house at Hinton Ampner exists now only in the stories inspired by events set down in an 18th-century manuscript.

In the British Library is the hand-written account of Mary Ricketts, tenant of that house from 1765 to 1772. Mary was married to William Henry Ricketts, a plantation owner, who spent a significant portion of his time in Jamaica. It was shortly after the Ricketts moved to Hinton Ampner with their children and household staff that the trouble began. Mary writes that 'soon after we were settled at Hinton I frequently heard noises in the night, as of people shutting, or rather slapping doors with vehemence'. At first it was assumed that the servants were responsible, or that there was some interloper who'd gained access to the house. But following interrogations, threats, dismissals and changes of the locks, the disturbances continued and became more severe.

Terrified, she summoned a maid to sit with her to listen for more footsteps.

In 1769, after Henry had left for his plantations, the presences made themselves far more conspicuously and terrifyingly felt. Mary writes about being roused from her sleep one night by the sound of heavy footsteps stumbling towards her bed but seeing no one. Terrified, she summoned a maid to sit with her to listen for more footsteps. They didn't come, but the women heard low groans and the sound of something rustling around the bed. Night and day the disturbances continued. There were unaccounted-for shrieks, disembodied muffled voices, the sound of running footsteps and spontaneously slamming doors. Two figures were said to materialise, one of a man in a long drab-coloured coat and one of a woman in a silk dress, the sort to make a rustling sound.

The humans in the house were becoming hysterical, but they weren't the only ones affected. Mary writes: 'One circumstance is of a nature so singularly striking that I cannot omit to relate it.

[...] I had frequently observed in a favourite cat that was usually in the parlour with me, and when sitting on table or chair with accustomed unconcern she would suddenly slink down as if struck with the greatest terror, conceal herself under my chair, and put her head close to my feet. [...] The servants gave the same account of a spaniel that lived in the house.'

Her husband away, the pets upset, her house servants leaving one by one, Mary called on her brother, Admiral Jervis, for help. He came with his friend, Captain Luttrell, and the two set up a vigil at the house. If nothing else, that night's events helped to convince Mary she wasn't alone in what she was experiencing, nor going mad. She didn't have the remedy to the situation, but she'd found the appropriate response, that 'the disturbances of the preceding night were of such a nature that the house was an unfit residence for any human being'.

The Ricketts moved out soon after and, the house having gained such a reputation, tenants were hard to find. The house was left empty until it was pulled down in 1793. During the demolition, workers made a grisly discovery – a box containing bones and what appeared to be the skull of an infant.

This unearthed memories of a scandal at Hinton Ampner, which had rocked the parish a few decades earlier. Edward Stawel had lived in the old Tudor house until his death from a sudden fit of apoplexy in the parlour in 1755. The rumour ran that Edward had had an affair with his sister-in-law Honoria, and a child was born to them but then mysteriously disappeared. Was the workers' discovery the sad fate of that child? And could the two apparitions have belonged to Edward and Honoria, tormented by grief or guilt over their wrongdoings?

Thankfully, the disturbances recorded by Mary Ricketts seem to have been confined to the old Tudor house and, now demolished, it can be considered a historic haunting. The National Trust now looks after Hinton Ampner, including the elegant neo-Georgian mansion built to replace the Tudor house. However, in 2014 the Trust did uncover the old house's foundations. There are some who have reported feelings of profound unease when they've been on the site of that old house – and of Mary's torment.

OXFORD CASTLE AND PRISON, OXFORDSHIRE

Norman in origin, by the Middle Ages Oxford Castle had been converted from a place that kept people out to one that kept people in. It also served as a court of justice, or assize, where sentences were handed down and executions carried out. The last person to be executed on this site was Oliver Butler (who was hanged for the murder of his girlfriend Rose Meadows in 1952) and prisoners were held here until 1996. The prison complex now operates as a tourist attraction, part of which has been imaginatively converted into a luxury hotel. The rooms afford every comfort in support of a good night's sleep, which certainly helps to distract from some of the nightmarish events of the prison's past.

In 1888, *Jackson's Oxford Journal* published a complete list of the executions that had taken place in the city in the previous

hundred years – 44 in total, all men. But executions had been carried out here for hundreds of years, and women were not exempt. One of the ghosts that haunts the castle is that of Mary Blandy, who was hanged in 1752 for poisoning her father.

Mary came from a wealthy family in Henley-on-Thames. When she came of marriageable age, her father, a lawyer and the town clerk, wanted only the best for his daughter and offered a dowry of £10,000 (over £2 million today). By doing this, he thought he'd be able to take his pick of the very finest suitors. One of the men who came forward was the son of a Scottish nobleman, but nobility is no guarantee of honesty. Captain William Henry Cranstoun began his courtship of Mary in 1746, and even managed to inveigle his way into the family home, but what he failed to reveal is that he'd already married in Scotland in 1744. When his secret was uncovered, and unwilling to give up his prize, Cranstoun tried, unsuccessfully, to have the earlier marriage annulled. Finally, in 1751, Mary's father, Francis, gave up on this opportunistic interloper and threw him out of the house.

Mary, unlike her father, was still very much enamoured with Cranstoun and it appears he manipulated her into doing a terrible thing. Cranstoun gave Mary some white powder, telling her it was a 'love philtre' that would soften her father's heart and make him forget his objection to them being together. Sure enough, some time later Francis became violently ill and took to his bed. His daughter brought him some tea and his condition deteriorated still further. Suspicion fell on his daughter, and perhaps she'd begun to suspect the powder wasn't helping matters, so Mary tried to dispose of the evidence. However, one of the household servants caught her in the act, had the powder tested and it was discovered that she had indeed, wittingly or not, been dosing her father with arsenic. The discovery came too late, and her father died in August 1751. Cranstoun fled but Mary was arrested and put on trial. She was convicted of her father's murder and hanged in April 1752. Her trial and execution caused a sensation – the story of a well-born woman stooping to such dastardly deeds inflaming the public's imagination.

He is a surly drunk and, aside from the bad language, he's been suspected of pulling the hair of visitors and being generally malevolent.

Another event at Oxford Castle, which created an even greater stir and much higher death toll, was the Black Assize of 1577. An assize held in the summer of that year included the trial of Rowland Jenkes for treason. He was found guilty, his sentence one of two imaginative forms of punishment – either to have his ears cut off or to be nailed to a pillory by his ears. As he was led away, he cursed the court. That curse, it was believed, manifested in a fatal illness that fell on everyone present that day, as recorded in a commemorative plaque of 1875: 'The Malady from the stench of the Prisoners developed itself during the Trial of one Rowland Jenkes, a saucy foul-mouthed Bookseller, for scandalous words uttered against the Queen.' Some have supposed an outbreak of typhus but as no women, children or paupers fell ill, a supernatural cause was suspected by many at the time.

Also foul-mouthed is the ghost of a 12th-century monk who dwells in the crypt below Oxford Castle. He has been heard making rude, and far from religious, utterances. The sauce in Brother Bernard's case was the beer he would brew here and drink in excess while his brothers prayed in the chapel above. Though no traces of Bernard's homebrew remain, visitors frequently comment on a distinct smell of alcohol in the crypt and some claim to have seen a cloaked monk slumped in what is now called Bernard's Corner. He is a surly drunk and, aside from the bad language, he's been suspected of pulling the hair of visitors and being generally malevolent. You'd think he'd be happier – as an eternal drunk, he'll never experience the hangover!

CLAYDON HOUSE, BUCKINGHAMSHIRE

It's often said that in war there are no winners. The Battle of Edgehill, the first key battle of the English Civil War, amply demonstrated that. It's thought the bloody skirmish that lasted an afternoon and evening left 500 Royalists and 500 Parliamentarians dead before being declared a draw.

One of those who died at Edgehill was Sir Edmund Verney of Claydon House. Sir Edmund was a passionate and very public supporter of Charles I. Though he didn't always agree with the king's politics, his loyalty to the Crown was unflinching, right up to the very end of his life, which was in active service to the king.

At the outbreak of the Civil War, in 1642, Sir Edmund was appointed standard bearer to the king. When Royalists and Parliamentarians clashed at Edgehill, he was 52 years old, but that didn't prevent him from reputedly killing 16 Parliamentarians before he was finally overcome. While it's difficult to verify this number, it's clear Sir Edmund attained legendary status. His was a heroic death, and it's said that he refused to surrender the royal standard, proclaiming, 'My life is my own, but the Standard is the King's!'

Some have described seeing a figure in 17th-century costume wandering on the first floor and looking quite distraught.

Sir Edmund was killed, his hand still grasping the standard. The Parliamentarians made off with it but the battle continued. With neither side able to overpower the other, when the Royalists reclaimed the standard, they found it with Sir Edmund's hand still attached, identified by his signet ring. His body was never recovered from the battlefield, but his hand was prised from the standard and given to the Verneys to be interred in the family vault at Claydon.

Many of the battle's dead were left where they fell. Just a couple of months after the conflict, shortly before the Christmas of 1642, villagers from nearby Kineton started seeing and hearing ghosts at the scene of the fray. There were so many sightings that two pamphlets were published in January 1643 detailing the phenomena. When news of this reached Charles I, he was sufficiently moved to send a Royal Commission to investigate, and it was determined that the corpses that still lay on the battlefield should be recovered and given Christian burials. This seems to have had the desired effect. The sightings reduced significantly at Edgehill, but Sir Edmund's ghost at Claydon House was granted no such release.

Over the centuries, there have been many sightings of Sir Edmund's ghost at Claydon House on the anniversary of his death at Edgehill, 23 October. Some have described seeing a figure in 17th-century costume wandering on the first floor, or sometimes on the stairs, looking quite distraught. It's believed this is the spirit of Sir Edmund, unable to rest either because his body wasn't recovered from the battlefield and buried, so his soul was unable to be committed to the afterlife in the proper way, or because he is in search of his missing hand.

CENTRAL ENGLAND AND EAST ANGLIA

COUGHTON COURT, WARWICKSHIRE

This book covers a wide variety of places – pubs and hotels, manor houses and moorland, castles and battlefields, palaces and prisons – and their stories are of ghosts of many colours. Women in white and grey feature prominently, but there's also one in pink, two women as well as two boys in blue, a woman in brown, four ladies and a small cohort of soldiers in green, and three black dogs. At Coughton (pronounced 'coat-un') Court there are said to be the ghosts of two women, also distinguished by their dresses, though little more than their apparent favourite colour is known about them.

Home to the Throckmorton family since the 15th century, this gracious Tudor house announces the importance of its family by the long, crenellated façade containing a grand three-storey gatehouse, lantern-like with leaded glass and boasting battlemented octagonal turrets. The Throckmortons still live in the house, though it has been in the ownership of the National Trust since 1946 and is open to the public in the summer months.

For any home to stay in the same family for 21 generations is impressive, but what is surprising is that, during their long involvement with the royal court, the Throckmortons did not always toe the line. They remained fervent Catholics during a period of history in which to do so meant persecution, and they even became involved in plots to overthrow the monarch, most famously the Gunpowder Plot of 1605.

The ringleader of the Gunpowder Plot was Robert Catesby, son of Sir William Catesby and Anne Throckmorton. Catesby recruited 12 other young Roman Catholic extremists to carry out his plan to blow up the House of Lords and the House of Commons, with James I and the entire Protestant government inside, during the State Opening of Parliament on 5 November of that year. One of Catesby's recruits was his cousin, Francis Tresham (see also page 78, Lyveden), who was the son of Sir Thomas Tresham and Muriel Throckmorton. As the planned date of the attack approached, Thomas Throckmorton prudently went abroad, but let out Coughton Court to Sir Everard Digby, one of the chief conspirators. As we all know, the plot was famously foiled and all 13 were put to death, but what is not known is quite how the Throckmortons managed to not only escape with their lives, but also retain their property.

As much of a mystery is the identity of the first of Coughton Court's colourful ghosts, the Pink Lady, who was said to haunt the area around the Tapestry Bedroom. And we're never likely to find out, as she was exorcised early in the 20th century, after which the sightings stopped.

Much more recent is the sighting of a woman's ghost in the churchyard of St Peter's Church, next to Coughton Court. In August 2014 a visitor, who describes herself as a sceptic of all things paranormal, saw a woman with long dark hair and wearing a golden-yellow dress. At first, she assumed it was a costumed interpreter of the kind often found at National Trust properties, but when the figure vanished before her eyes she was understandably shaken. When she went inside the property, to her further amazement she saw the same woman staring down at her from a portrait of Lucy Throckmorton, painted *c*.1700.

And so Coughton Court gives us the Yellow Lady to add to our game of 'ghost snooker'.

BADDESLEY CLINTON, WARWICKSHIRE

Built in the 15th century, Baddesley Clinton, like so many houses in the care of the National Trust, has been home to a procession of generations. These people lived within its walls, imbuing them with the events of their lives, and many will have died here, perhaps also leaving traces of their passing. Some will have gone quietly, no doubt, but it's possible that some will have been bundled more violently off this mortal coil, given the turbulent history to which this house was witness – for the

Ferrers were Catholics at a time when to hold that belief meant persecution and possible death.

Considering the very real life-and-death dramas that played out at Baddesley Clinton, it's perhaps unsurprising that it has become the backdrop of many a ghost story. One of the first to document uncanny goings-on at Baddesley Clinton was Rebecca Ferrers, who lived here with her husband Marmion in the second half of the late 19th century. She wrote: 'I once heard that solemn tread. It had an indescribably awful and mournful sound ... and affected me deeply.... It had a very weird effect to hear the handle jerked loudly within a few feet of where you are standing and see no-one.' When others reported hearing footsteps and seeing handles being turned – some even claimed to see an apparition of a man in a red jacket with a white belt across his chest – Rebecca investigated. When she came across a miniature of Major Thomas Ferrers, who died on active service in France in 1817, in a uniform matching that description, she determined it was his ghost who was stalking the corridor of the upper landing and had an exorcism performed.

When her mother came back a little later to check on her and asked what she had been doing, the girl replied that she had been playing with the lady dressed in grey.

But there were still more restless spirits, the one most reported being that of a lady in grey. In the 1920s, a cleaning lady brought her daughter to Baddesley Clinton, leaving the child to amuse herself while she worked. When her mother came back a little later to check on her and asked what she had been doing, the girl replied that she had been playing with the lady dressed in grey. There was nobody else in the house. Then in the 1990s, two National Trust volunteers were closing up when one of them saw a figure of a woman carrying a lighted candle. The other volunteer was alerted to the sight, but the figure had disappeared. When the two reported this to staff, they were told there was no one in the house and candles were not permitted anywhere in the property.

Humans can be unreliable witnesses, it's true, but what about animals? Are they so affected by their imaginations, or compelled simply to make stuff up to gain their owner's attention? In the 1930s, a Jack Russell would frequent Baddesley Clinton with its owner. Whenever they were in the Great Hall, the dog would sit and beg in front of the same empty chair, so much so that the family came to call it the 'ghost's chair'.

Since Baddesley Clinton came into the care of the National Trust, dogs haven't been allowed in the house, except for assistance dogs. In the early 2000s, one such dog, generally the most biddable and compliant of canines, refused to enter Henry Ferrers' bedroom and none of the usual commands or treats would make the dog change its mind. This same room has caused visitors to comment that they've felt suddenly cold when entering and one even had to leave when they felt a spontaneous wave of depression.

Unexplained occurrences have long been reported at Baddesley Clinton and, while it's true its romantic appearance and intriguing history stir the imagination, there are yet lingering mysteries attached to this place that defy explanation.

DUDLEY CASTLE, WEST MIDLANDS

This destination of haunted repute is another castle, or at least what's left of it. Castles feature heavily in our ghostly tour, which is hardly surprising as we expect the most haunted places in Britain to be the ones that have stood for longest, with the lives and the loves, the tragedies and the torments, and the unfinished business of its inhabitants bound up in their walls.

There is Beaumaris Castle where the spirits of soldiers, labourers and monks have imbued the place with their blood, sweat and prayers (see page 143); Ballygally Castle where a noblewoman died an ignoble death plummeting from her turret-room window (see page 148); Dunluce Castle where star-crossed lovers drowned by moonlight (see page 156); Culzean Castle where its lost piper still plays and a tortured cleric still screams out in fear and pain (see page 164); Crathes Castle and the fateful consequences of forbidden love (see page 178); Bamburgh Castle with its wraiths in pink and green (see page 114); Chillingham Castle with its many victims of one of the most sadistic men who ever lived (see page 117); Lumley Castle where religious persecution forced poor Lily down a well (see page 128); the Tower of London where queens, lords and ladies were cut down to size (see page 34); and Oxford Castle, haunted by a poisoner and a drunken monk (see page 49).

Of the castles listed above, Dudley and Dunluce have the most ruined appearance, with Beaumaris also something of a shell, as an unfinished building project. When visiting ruins, our imaginations must work that bit harder to comprehend how the buildings once fitted together, and how they might have looked and functioned. With our minds set to filling in the gaps, could that explain the disproportionate number of paranormal sightings at these places?

The reports of apparitions at Dudley Castle are certainly many and various, perhaps due to the curiosity and open minds its visitors bring with them. These days, of course, they also bring their phones with them, and when a couple visiting the castle in October 2014 captured an image of what they believed to be Dudley's best-known ghost, the Grey Lady, framed in a doorway onto the castle's courtyard, it made the mainstream media. Many took this to be proof of paranormal activity. But what it proves beyond doubt is that interest in ghosts endures even in this modern age, and the belief, or at least a desire to believe, in

something in the hereafter is quite common. (An Ispos MORI poll of 2017 revealed 38 per cent of respondents classified themselves as believing in ghosts, and a similar number reported that they'd seen one.)

Of the many ghostly sightings reported at Dudley Castle, the Grey Lady is one of just two to be named. She's believed to be the spirit of Dorothy Beaumont, the wife of Lieutenant Colonel John Beaumont who was stationed at the castle during the English Civil War. He and his wife are in the records as having a child 'borne and buryd' on the same day in 1644. The infant was buried in a church located outside the castle walls, but when Dorothy passed away a couple of years later her wish to be buried alongside her child was not possible as the castle was at the time under siege by the Parliamentarians. Cruelly separated from her baby both in life and in death, Dorothy's ghost now restlessly roams the ruins of the castle.

This sad story is a local legend and at Dudley Castle tours feature costumed actors performing as the Grey Lady. On one occasion, visitors were curious to know why there were two actresses on the castle keep, made more curious still when they were told there is only ever one person employed to act the role.

The other named ghost at Dudley Castle is John de Somery. John died in 1322 and his body is believed to have been interred in a large sarcophagus in the undercroft beneath the castle's chapel. His spectre has, you could say, a small walk-on part compared to the Grey Lady's, according to one witness report. A cleaner was working in the undercroft one day when she suddenly saw a pair of legs in thigh-high riding boots standing by the stone coffin. She was further alarmed when her eyes travelled upwards but saw no upper body.

Both Dorothy Beaumont and John de Somery are in the castle's historical records, but there are many reports of other figures and apparitions belonging to nameless individuals. Their anonymity doesn't make their manifestations seem any less real to the people who've experienced them. They are a poignant reminder that many lives may not make a mark on the public record, but their personal traumas and disappointments are enough to leave an imprint somewhere between the physical and spiritual worlds.

CANNOCK CHASE, STAFFORDSHIRE

This destination is one that serves a vital function to the many people who live in the towns and cities that surround it. Designated as an Area of Outstanding Natural Beauty in 1958, Cannock Chase may be the smallest of the AONBs, but its 26 square miles of heathland, oak woodland, pine forests, walking and cycling trails, rivers and canals offer an estimated 2.5 million visitors a year fresh air and adventure in natural surroundings. There's biking, hiking, Nordic walking, horse riding, dog sledding, tree-top adventures – it really is bursting with activities.

If all this is sounding very wholesome, then it's worth noting that Cannock Chase is also believed to be a portal to another world. There is little that is supernatural that has not been spotted on the Chase – werewolves, black dogs, UFOs, big cats and a giant hairy creature with blazing red eyes ('Team called in over Bigfoot sightings', *Birmingham Mail*, 14 February 2006). The area has been subject to extensive investigations, and it has been noted that it lies on the intersection of two ley lines. The distribution of the various sightings suggests the epicentre of Cannock Chase's supernatural activity is at Castle Ring, an Iron Age hill fort where a tribe known as the Cornovii would have performed rituals, thought to have included blood sacrifices.

Now, the last time we saw this much supernatural activity in one place was The Ancient Ram Inn (see page 27). That accursed pub is similarly situated on the intersection of two ley lines and, perhaps more pointedly, on a site where an ancient people carried out human sacrifices. Coincidence?

Some have said they've felt as though they were being hypnotised, her black eyes being the feature that witnesses have most focused on.

The most famous of Cannock Chase's ghosts is the Black-Eyed Child, with reported sightings beginning in the 1970s. She's said to appear suddenly, calling out for help in a childlike voice, but when people have approached her, they've become overwhelmed with fear. Some have said they've felt as though they were being hypnotised, her black eyes without whites or irises being the feature that witnesses have most focused on.

Another ghost in the woods is thought to be that of Henry Paget, 1st Marquess of Anglesey. The Paget family home was Beaudesert, which stood on the south-eastern edge of Cannock

Chase and was said to be his favourite hunting ground. (An irresistible footnote to any mention of the 1st Marquess of Anglesey is that, when badly wounded by a cannonball at the Battle of Waterloo, he is said to have exclaimed to Wellington: 'By God, sir, I've lost my leg!' to which Wellington replied, 'By God, sir, so you have!')

On the opposite edge of Cannock Chase is Shugborough Hall, owned by the National Trust and thought to be haunted by two ghosts – a housekeeper and a former lady of the house who died in childbirth. Given that Shugborough derives from the Old English word *scucca*, meaning 'goblin' or 'demon', and *burgh* meaning 'hill', the hall is getting off lightly with just two.

Also wandering the woods at Cannock Chase is the ghost of an old man who carries a cane and wears a wide-brimmed hat, thought to be a former gamekeeper. Ghostly soldiers have been seen running; a parachutist endlessly falling from the sky; a cyclist vanishing into thin air.... The ghosts of the departed really are as active as visitors to the Chase today.

HIGH PEAK ESTATE, DERBYSHIRE

The Peak District has been a National Park since 1951, and the first to be designated as such. It's a place millions flock to each year for recreation, savouring its wildness, its remoteness, its exposure to all the elements – all the things that have been the undoing of many an unwary traveller in times past. Check the forecast, charge your phone, bring the right gear – 'There's no such thing as bad weather, only unsuitable clothing' – and the Peaks pose no particular peril. Yet judging by the number of local tales told about a variety of unfortunate souls, you may still be in for a surprise for which no amount of packing can prepare you.

The Peak District is a park of two halves – the White Peak and the Dark Peak. Dark Peak is an alternative name for High Peak and is the higher, wilder and more northerly part of the park. The name comes from its geology that causes the soil in winter to be almost always saturated with water, making it largely uninhabitable with any hollows filled with bog moss and black peat. Its desolation and lack of habitation mean that, should you be unfortunate enough to slip, get caught in a storm or be waylaid by some brigand, there would be no one to hear your cries, at least not in time to come to your aid ....

There are some who say they have heard the plaintive cries of two tragic lovers, who long ago passed this way to be married, but who were united instead in a most brutal death. The tale dates back to the mid-1750s and has been told countless times since. Perhaps the earliest published account was in the 28 April 1788 edition of the *Derby News*, which reported that the remains of two people had been discovered in 1768 by some miners sinking an engine pit. This gruesome discovery had remained a mystery until, 10 years later, one James Ashton made a deathbed confession to a double murder. The details of his confession, combined with local accounts of a couple who had gone missing in the area, added up to this grisly tale.

The story goes that, in 1758, a woman named Clara from a wealthy family fell in love with a penniless labourer, sometimes named as Henry, more often as Alan, so we'll go with the latter. Clara's family disapproved of the match, so she and Alan decided to elope. At the time, there was a chapel in Peak Forest that had the unusual condition of being exempt from episcopal jurisdiction, meaning the minister could grant marriage licences without reference to the bishop. On their way to the chapel to be married, Clara and Alan decided to stay the night at an inn in Castleton. While taking refreshment and presumably making plans for their future, the couple unwittingly sealed their fate. Being from a wealthy family, Clara's dress and deportment had attracted the attention of a group of ne'er-do-wells. As Clara and Alan excitedly discussed their plans, these men made their own and, knowing exactly the route their victims would be taking, lay in wait for them the following day.

Early the next morning, the five men were waiting for Clara and Alan at Winnats Pass. It's a spectacular limestone gorge, a spot that will take your breath away, and this is certainly how it went for the young couple. The five men leapt upon them and pulled Clara and Alan from their horses. Their intent was surely always murderous, as the men had with them the means to bury the bodies, which lay in their shallow graves until miners stumbled upon them a decade later. The couple's horses were found wandering a few days later, which led locals to realise something untoward had happened to Clara and Alan. There was widespread suspicion of exactly who the culprits were but no evidence to go on. However, while the murderous miscreants seemed to have got away with it, the local legend goes on to suggest that each met a miserable end, as if under some inescapable curse. The confessor, James Ashton, went mad and died in poverty; Francis Butler also went mad and died within a year of the couple's disappearance; Thomas Hall hanged himself; Nicholas Cook fell to his death from a precipice near the murder scene; and John Bradshaw was again at Winnats Pass when a boulder fell, crushing the life out of him.

Clara and Alan may have had their young lives cruelly cut short, just as they were about to embark on a new one together, but here on the High Peak they have not been forgotten. There are reminders both physical and metaphysical. Clara's red leather saddle was for a while displayed in a local pub and can now be seen at the Speedwell Cavern Museum. Since the time of their disappearance and over the next 250 years, locals have told of blood-curdling screams emanating from somewhere in the pass. On windy nights, it's said that the couple's pleas for mercy can be heard. There have

There have also been reports of two people desperately scrambling up the rocky slopes of Winnats Pass only to disappear into thin air.

also been reports of two people desperately scrambling up the rocky slopes of Winnats Pass only to disappear into thin air. Wherever Clara and Alan are, at least they are together.

Lifelong devotion seems a popular theme in these parts, and certainly it's true that wherever and whenever you walk in the Peak District, you should never walk alone. But companions can come in all guises, and not all of them human. Several monuments can be found on the moors marking where farmers or shepherds met their ends, their dogs steadfastly by their side. Take Tip, the most famous of them all, who stayed by her master's body for 105 days after the pair were caught up in a vicious blizzard in December 1953.

Also immortalised, by monument and by myth, is the Lost Lad. There is a cairn near Derwent Edge that marks the spot where a shepherd boy and his dog perished in a snowstorm. The boy's name was Abraham Lowe – the dog's name is not recorded – and the pair went missing while out on the moors trying to retrieve the family's flock before the weather turned. Abraham took shelter beneath a rock but to no avail and hypothermia claimed him. Months later, a shepherd spotted the words 'Lost Lad' scratched into the rock and there, huddled together, were the remains of the boy and his dog, who had refused to leave his master's side. This sad tale moved locals, who started leaving a stone whenever they passed by the spot as a mark of respect, creating the cairn that has become known as the Lost Lad.

Ever since, sightings of the ghosts of Abraham and his dog have been reported by farmers and hikers at this spot in mid-winter, particularly when snow is threatening. In 1983, a school teacher from Manchester reported seeing the pair. He called out, received no reply, and then they vanished.

Another disappearing dog, but this one much more of the prowling, slavering, cattle-bothering variety, has been reported on the High Peak. Phantom dogs are as popular in the folklore of the Peak District as anywhere else, the myths doubtless originating in the fact that wolves did indeed once roam these moors. However, they proved irresistible sport to some and were hunted to extinction in the UK by the second half of the 18th century. So, when a newspaper ran reports in the 1920s of a huge black dog that had been attacking and killing sheep in the area around the village of Edale, this could have been no wolf.

In the 1950s, encounters with an unearthly black dog were still being reported by locals, so Scottish writer Alasdair Alpin MacGregor came to investigate. He met with and interviewed one Greta Shirt, the daughter of a farmer and an extremely brave young woman. She told him how she had been walking home one night when she clearly saw, by the light of the moon, a huge black dog. As it came closer, she put out a hand to stroke it but found that her hand touched only air and the dog had passed straight through a wire fence. When she got home and told her father what had happened, he was unsurprised and admitted he had seen the ghost dog himself, saying: 'I'll admit there is a black ghost dog along there, but I did not want to tell you until you were grown out of childhood.'

From wild beasts in the wilds of the High Peak to a very different sort of place, once described as 'robust, unostentatious, dignified and a trifle prim'. That it may be, but that formal façade hides a very dark secret ....

GUNBY, LINCOLNSHIRE

Gunby Hall appears as a grand town house but dropped into a secluded setting at the end of a half-mile-long private drive in the middle of the Lincolnshire countryside. The overall effect is of an exceedingly pretty but modestly sized country house. The main body of the house was built in 1700 for the Massingberd family, where generations of that family lived up until the 1960s, the last of them, Lady Montgomery-Massingberd, having donated the estate to the National Trust in 1944.

This pattern of ownership is not unusual – wealthy families created country seats to pass down the generations, but a series of seismic social shifts in the 20th century made staffing difficult, maintenance unaffordable and inheritance problematic, and so a great many estates were donated to the National Trust. What is more unusual is Gunby's tradition of inheritance down the female line. There is a story of a sinister nature that exists to explain how this might have come to pass.

In the early 1700s, there was a coachman who – far exceeding his station – was discovered to be having an affair with a lady of the house. Accounts vary, with some saying it was Sir William Massingberd's daughter and others saying it was his wife. In either case, this was too much for Sir William to bear. On the night that the two lovers planned to run away together, Sir William jumped out from his place of hiding and shot the coachman dead, before dragging his body to the pond where it was unceremoniously dumped.

Sir William's immediate problem was solved but his actions, according to some, were to have unforeseen consequences. He may have thought he had got away with the murder, but word must have spread. Soon locals were whispering that Gunby was cursed due to some grievous deed, which meant that no male of Massingberd descent would ever inherit the house.

Sir William's son, another William, did inherit from his father in 1719, but he died unmarried just four years later. So began the family tradition of female succession, with William's sister, Elizabeth. Her husband combined her name with his, so their son, William Meux-Massingberd, inherited Gunby and held it for a lengthy period, during which time he married twice. He had many children, but only one son, who predeceased him.

In the absence of a son and heir, the estate passed to a grandson. He died when his only daughter was just a baby; she was raised elsewhere but, when she came of age, she married and settled at Gunby.

So it wasn't quite true to say no male of Massingberd descent would ever inherit the house, but it certainly wasn't straightforward for them. Indeed, some wouldn't even consider it a curse. Certainly not Emily Langton-Massingberd, who inherited Gunby in 1887, by which time she'd already made a name for herself as a women's rights campaigner.

Members of the Massingberd family enjoyed Gunby for many years after the so-called curse, creating a beautiful home and laying out spectacular gardens, finally gifting it to the National Trust so it could be enjoyed by many more generations to come. The only person for whom it worked out badly was the coachman, whose ghost has been seen on the path by the pond, now known as Ghost Walk.

NEWSTEAD ABBEY, NOTTINGHAMSHIRE

Given its modern-day appearance as part romantic ruin, part glamorously Gothic country house, its history as the home of the legendary Romantic poet Lord Byron and its origins as an Augustinian monastery, it's little wonder that ghost stories about Newstead Abbey abound.

The abbey ceased to be, along with so many others, during the Dissolution of the Monasteries. That took place in the 1530s but the monks of Newstead Abbey persisted, in spiritual form at least, and there are many stories of their appearances, including one that dates from the 1930s. A doctor had been summoned to a house in Newstead village where a woman was in labour. When he eventually arrived, the panicked father-to-be demanded to know what had taken him so long. The doctor replied that he had struggled to find the address and had to ask for directions, which he received from a black-robed figure in the grounds of the abbey who had silently pointed the way.

Another story about an encounter with a former brother of the abbey dates to Lord Byron's time at Newstead and describes something far more confrontational. The Goblin Friar had been known to the Byron family for some time as a portent of disaster. Lord Byron is as famous for his love affairs as for his poems, but he did briefly marry – an episode he later described as the unhappiest of his life. So it was on the eve of his wedding that Lord Byron awoke to the sight of the Goblin Friar climbing onto his bed, watching him with baleful eyes that burned red.

Terrified though he must have been, Byron did not heed the warning and went on to marry, divorcing a year later.

Where Byron did succeed in finding a life partner was with his adored dog, Boatswain. There is a large monument to Boatswain in the grounds of Newstead Abbey that bears the poem 'Epitaph to a Dog'. This deeply moving eulogy to Byron's best friend contains the lines: 'But the poor Dog, in life the firmest friend, / The first to welcome, foremost to defend, / Whose honest heart is still his Master's own, / Who labours, fights, lives, breathes for him alone, / Unhonour'd falls, unnotic'd all his worth, / Deny'd in heaven the Soul he held on earth.' Some believe Boatswain's soul still resides here at Newstead, his ghost prowling the grounds, looking for his master, whose wishes to be buried beside his dog were ignored.

Between his divorce aged 28 and his death aged 36, Byron had years of chaotic escapades, partly funded by the sale of Newstead Abbey in 1818. It was bought by an old school friend of Byron's, Thomas Wildman, and it was during the time he lived here with his wife that a tragic event gave rise to Newstead Abbey's White Lady.

By the 1820s, Byron was the Regency equivalent of a rock star. His fame and ability to make women swoon at a hundred paces were unsurpassed. He had fans everywhere, including Sophie Hyatt who lived near Newstead. When the Wildmans learned how keen she was on Byron and his work, they allowed her to visit the abbey gardens whenever she liked. In time they must have grown fond of the girl as, when they heard she had fallen on hard times, Mrs Wildman sent her a note inviting her to come live with them. However, before the note could reach her, Sophie was run over and killed by a horse and cart. Unable

to accept the invitation in life, she has since taken up permanent residence at Newstead Abbey in the form of the White Lady and continues to visit her beloved gardens, most often seen along a path known as White Lady's Walk.

LYVEDEN, NORTHAMPTONSHIRE

Lyveden cuts a very melancholic figure against the skyline of a remote and rural part of Northamptonshire. The ambition behind this building begun in 1595 is clear to see, but work on it was abandoned in 1605 on the death of Sir Thomas Tresham. It should have been beautiful – elaborate Elizabethan water gardens, the journey through which would have culminated in a moated lodge full of symbolism proclaiming its designer's Catholic faith – but it remains the most forlorn site.

Whether due to its remoteness or its appearance as a totem of bad luck, Lyveden has remained virtually untouched for centuries. Visitors did venture this way, before the National Trust took it into its care in 1922, and left their mark on the place in the form of graffiti scratched into the masonry. Some of these marks suggest that people did indeed think some sort of a hex was on this place, as they include symbols that were believed to protect against evil spirits, such as a six-petalled design known as a 'daisy wheel' or 'hexafoil'.

The best-known ghost story involving Lyveden centres on what is believed to be an unmarked grave in the Middle Garden, also known as the Moated Garden. Scottish novelist and poet George Whyte-Melville lived in Northamptonshire for a time in the mid-19th century and learned of the story. Whyte-Melville was known more for his interest in field sports than ghost stories, but this one may have piqued his interest as it concerned the fate of some of his countrymen a century earlier, one in particular who never left Lyveden. He writes: 'On the wayside turf that borders the tract of woodland stretching between Brigstock and Oundle is a low green mound called the Soldier's Grave. The natives of the district do not care to pass it after dark for of course the place is haunted, and a figure is sometimes said to be seen sitting on the mound in the dusk, shrouded in a long dark mantle.'

In 1743, most of Europe's great powers were three years into the War of the Austrian Succession. George II needed more bodies on the battlefield, so he summoned the 42nd Regiment of Foot, later known as the Black Watch, from Edinburgh to London. There was reluctance among the regiment and Scottish officials, who reminded the government of the understanding that the services of the Black Watch should be confined to Scotland. They were told the king wanted only to inspect them, but when they got to London and were told they were to be shipped off to Flanders, around 100 members of the Black Watch mutinied.

Led by Corporals Malcolm and Samuel MacPherson and Private Farquhar Shaw, they set out for Scotland and, after walking for seven days, got as far as Ladywood on the outskirts of Oundle. This is thought to have been within Lyveden's water gardens. There, exhausted and hungry, they decided their capture and punishment (invariably by firing squad) were inevitable, so better to alert the authorities before they caught up with them, and negotiate a pardon.

Over the course of two days, they negotiated through a local Justice of the Peace with the Duke of Montagu as the king's representative and at that time the largest land owner in Northamptonshire. The duke's pardon for all men in return for their surrender was not forthcoming, and on the third day they were surprised and captured by a company of the King's Dragoons. All except the three taken to be the ringleaders and one other were shipped off to garrisons in Jamaica, Gibraltar and Menorca, with the remainder sent to fight at Flanders. The MacPhersons and Shaw were executed by firing squad at the Tower of London (see page 34). The one other is an unnamed soldier, who died of hunger and exhaustion at Lyveden, and who was buried beneath the mound where his ghost sometimes appears.

WICKEN FEN, CAMBRIDGESHIRE

Continuing eastwards we enter the Kingdom of the East Angles, famed for fenland and farmland, and for a while the most powerful Anglo-Saxon kingdom of England. Vestiges of its ancient history can be found throughout the region, on its coast and rivers, in its towns and cities, and in its stories and folklore.

For much of that history, the landscape of the area looked very different. Wicken Fen is a rare survivor indeed. Fenland, the low-lying marshland around the estuary of the Wash, used to extend as far north as Lincoln and as far south as Cambridge. It took centuries of human industriousness and ingenuity to re-engineer the landscape and pump it dry for the planting of crops. Before the 19th century it was a much wilder landscape, a place on the limits of the land and the sea, which was under water for a great part of the year, and home to those who were wise to its changing ways and ever-present dangers.

Unsurprisingly then, featuring large in East Anglia's folklore are tales that urged great caution when out on the fens. You had to be alert to all the sights and sounds of nature if you wanted to make it safely across, and of course many didn't. As with any wilderness, fenland can be disorientating, and with the knowledge that a misstep could be fatal, locals sensed a malevolence about the place, a malevolence that was given a name – the Lantern Man.

The Lantern Man lurks on the fens, biding his time, waiting for unwary travellers. The light in the lantern that he carries flickers and flits about in a way that no human moves. Is this an unnatural force, or is it a spirit of nature? Some people liken him to the phenomenon of will-o'-the-wisp, a ghost light seen by travellers at night, especially over bogs, swamps or marshes. But unlike will-o'-the-wisp, which is said to lure the unsuspecting to unsafe ground where they meet a sticky end, the Lantern Man will come for you! He's particularly attuned to whistling, as one survivor reported who was trying to attract the attention of his dog but instead found himself fleeing from the Lantern Man. In 1900, *Eastern Counties* magazine published a piece of advice to help people escape the clutches of the Lantern Man: travel in pairs but at a good distance from each other, so if you draw the Lantern Man's attention, you take it in turns to whistle, luring him this way and that until you can get to safety. Another survival strategy is to fall to the ground, bury your face in the mud and hold your breath until he's gone away.

And if you thought carrying a torch would be a good idea, to scare away any evil spirits lurking in the dark, think again, as there are reports of the Lantern Man actually running towards the light. Walter Rye was an athlete and antiquary who wrote many books about East Anglia and as the 'father of cross-country running' would have spent much of his time outdoors. In 1870 he wrote about a man who had encountered the Lantern Man, dropped his own light and run for his life. When he ventured to look back, there was the Lantern Man kicking the lantern over and over again.

Walter Rye is a source of other paranormal perils that you'd do well to be aware of when out and about in the area, especially after dark. Many regions have stories of unfeasibly sized phantom dogs, and East Anglia's is called Black Shuck, often described as being unusually large, with black shaggy fur and red blazing eyes. Rye described an encounter in which a man was knocked off his feet by something invisible, but then was aware of something slinking away, with eyes like bicycle lamps. Writer and naturalist William Alfred Dutt gives a fuller description in his 1901 *Highways & Byways in East Anglia*: 'He takes the form of a huge black dog, and prowls along dark lanes and lonesome field footpaths, where, although his howling makes the hearer's blood run cold, his footfalls make no sound. You may know him at once, should you see him, by his fiery eye; he has but one, and that, like the Cyclops', is in the middle of his head. But such an encounter might bring you the worst of luck: it's even said that to meet him is to be warned that your death will occur before the end of the year. So you will do well to shut your eyes if you hear him howling; shut them even if you are uncertain whether it's the dog fiend or the voice of the wind you hear.'

So don't whistle or carry a torch, but do bury your face in the mud, hold your breath and close your eyes. Got that? Good. On we go to our next property.

RAYNHAM HALL, NORFOLK

Raynham Hall, unlike our other destinations, is not generally open to the public, but rather hosts occasional recitals and open days. However, it's included here as, from 1835 and for the next one hundred years, the hall was allegedly the haunt of the Brown Lady, whose fame culminated with the publication of one of the most famous ghost photographs of all time.

The first sighting of the Brown Lady was at Christmas 1835. The owner of the hall at the time, Charles Townshend, had invited a number of guests to join in the festivities. On approaching their bedrooms one night, two of the guests claimed to have seen an apparition of a woman in an old-fashioned dress with brown brocade. The next night they saw her again and, perhaps being less startled this time, were able to study her in more detail and noted her hollow eye sockets.

It was concluded that this was the ghost of Dorothy (second wife of Charles Townshend, 2nd Viscount Townshend), who lived at Raynham Hall until her mysterious death in 1726, aged just 40. There were already rumours about Dorothy's premarital affair with the politician Lord Wharton and her unhappy marriage to the quick-tempered Charles 'Turnip' Townshend. So it wasn't difficult for the story to take hold that her husband had discovered she was continuing her affair with Lord Wharton, locked her up and left her to slowly waste away.

The following year, the story having already garnered considerable attention, Captain Frederick Marryat, a friend of Charles Dickens and a novelist himself, asked to stay the night at Raynham Hall in its most haunted room. Marryat had been a Royal Navy officer and specialised in fiction of a nautical bent. He had developed a theory that the haunting was nothing more than a story concocted by smugglers to keep people away from the area.

His stay lasted three nights and, as a naval man with a conspiracy theory about smugglers, he kept a revolver under his pillow. On the first two nights he saw nothing. On his last night, however, he heard and saw someone moving around the upstairs corridors by lamplight. These details and what happened next we know from an account written by Marryat's daughter, Florence, also an author. He kept himself hidden from view until the figure was close enough to be recognisable as the Brown Lady. As she drew level with him, she held the lamp up to her face and grinned at the captain. Here Florence picks up the story: 'This act so infuriated my father, who was anything but lamb-like in disposition, that he sprang into the corridor with a bound, and discharged the revolver right in her face.'

After this encounter sightings dwindled, with the next one not reported until 1926. What got everyone talking about the Brown Lady again was the photograph published by *Country Life* after an assignment at Raynham Hall on 19 September 1936. As one of the most beautiful houses in England, its architectural glories were what photographer Captain Hubert C. Provand went to capture, but his shot of an ethereal, veiled form gliding down the hall's main staircase drew huge public attention. As it happened, it wasn't entirely unwanted attention, as the lady of the house at the time, Gwladys, Dowager Marchioness Townshend, had just published a book about haunted houses, in which Raynham Hall took centre stage.

BLICKLING HALL, NORFOLK

This Jacobean mansion was built on the ruins of a Tudor hall. To this house, though she would not recognise it, its most famous ghost returns each year, risen from arguably the most ruinous period of English history. In fact, each year not only she but also her brother and her father return to Blickling Hall. The events of her life had such a huge impact on history that, fittingly, her and her family's appearances on the anniversary of her death are recorded as dramatic in the extreme.

She was Anne Boleyn, Queen of England from 1533 to 1536 and Henry VIII's second wife. It was Henry's wish to divorce his first wife and marry Anne that created the schism between the Church of England and the Roman Catholic Church, reinforcing the political and ideological differences that contributed to centuries of near constant war between the

countries of Europe and even between people of the same country, the same community.

It's believed that Anne and her siblings, Mary and George, were born at Blickling, and they lived here with their parents, Thomas and Elizabeth Boleyn. Thomas was a diplomat and politician in the court of Henry VIII, who worked hard to gain the king's favour, gaining titles along the way, but his greatest achievement – which he will have done everything to promote – must have been when he saw his daughter married to a king. Until she fell from favour.

On 15 May 1536 Anne was found guilty of treason, having been accused of pursuing extramarital affairs with five men, including her brother George. On 19 May, she was beheaded by a skilled swordsman brought over from France specially for the occasion – her husband granting a mercy so small you couldn't cut it with the sharpest blade. Her brother was also beheaded, but with an axe. Since then, on that very date, the gore-spattered ghosts of Anne, George and Thomas Boleyn have all been sighted at Blickling.

Anne arrives at night in a carriage drawn by four headless horses, driven by a headless horseman. She wears white and clutches her head as she's seated in the carriage, before she dismounts, blood dripping down her dress, and enters the hall to spend the hours until daybreak wandering through its rooms. Her brother George's appearance is far less processional. It's his misfortune on that night to be dragged around the surrounding countryside by four headless horses. Finally, their father's ghost performs its guilty penance for Thomas's failure to save his children: every year and for a thousand years his ghost must drive his spectral coach and phantom horses over the dozen bridges between Wroxham and Blickling before the break of dawn and the cock's crow.

These much-recounted sightings are incredible enough, but more incredible still, they're not Blickling Hall's only ghosts.

In 1616, the Boleyns' reputation and family seat both in ruins, Sir Henry Hobart, 1st Baronet, built the mansion you see today. In time, it was inherited by the 4th baronet, another Sir Henry, who had a reasonably successful political career – MP for King's Lynn, Thetford and Norfolk but lost St Ives – but who is perhaps better known for being killed in a duel. It's suggested that he had a reputation for being a somewhat quarrelsome man, particularly over land disputes. However, on this occasion, the argument arose when this Sir Henry discovered that someone had been spreading rumours of him being a coward during a military campaign in Ireland. He challenged the slanderer, one Oliver Le Neve, met him on

Cawston Heath, was fatally wounded and died the next day in a turret bedroom in Blickling Hall.

That should be where Sir Henry's story ended, but a local legend has preserved a gruesome epilogue about the fate of a squire of Blickling who 'dared to taint the fair spot with wickedness so great that none could speak of it'. In his 1926 book *Round About Norfolk and Suffolk*, F.J. Meyrick relates how, when Sir Henry's body was laid to rest in the graveyard at Blickling church, a stray dog came whining to the graveside. No more might have been said about his interment, but that the very next day the body had been exhumed: 'It was a strange and dreadful resurrection! Mother Earth had refused her son. The very corpse of the buried nobleman had been torn from its casket of lead and lay there poisoning the June day.' They tried burying him elsewhere, in unconsecrated ground. The same thing happened again. It was then decided that the body be taken to the lake, weighted down with stones and thrown in.

A week passed without the body resurfacing, but then the estate's keeper fished a huge black eel out of the lake. Eels were once common in the rivers and lakes of East Anglia and on East Anglian dinner tables, so the keeper took this prize catch to Blickling Hall's cook. What happened next was extraordinary.

> *A week passed without the body resurfacing, but then the estate's keeper fished a huge black eel out of the lake.*

Once in the kitchen, the eel transpired to be a black, wet dog with, so the story goes, the dead man's eyes. The dog proceeded to prowl about the estate and no one could get close to it. Just a few pages back we were introduced to Black Shuck (see page 80, Wicken Fen). Every estate worker would have been very familiar with this phantom hound and absolutely terrified.

So they did what any person would do in this situation, they invited a famous wizard up from London. That wizard performed a ritual to bring the beast to heel and was able to lead it to the master's room in the turret, which the village mason promptly bricked up.

But the story doesn't even end there, as Meyrick goes on to tell of an event that was witnessed by his father, who was Blickling's rector in the 1860s and visiting the then squire's sisters. Suddenly, one of the sisters cried out, convinced that she'd seen a large black dog run across the drawing room and hide behind a tapestry. The rector said he'd seen nothing but, so unnerved by what she thought she'd seen, she asked her sister if she'd seen it and they went looking for the dog. They found nothing.

The next morning, the squire, who knew nothing of the mysterious apparition in the drawing room, revealed that he had had the turret room opened up just the day before. Had he unleashed Sir Henry's hellish familiar, gone to join the packs of phantom black dogs that roam about East Anglia?

From unhelpful disturbances that break out of the ethereal realm, on now to spirits that offer more in the way of guidance.

SUTTON HOO, SUFFOLK

Sutton Hoo is famous the world over for the discovery of what has so often been described as a 'ghost ship', but what was actually unearthed here was so much more than that. By the end of the summer of 1939, an Anglo-Saxon Royal Burial Ground containing grave goods of unrivalled quality had been uncovered, only for work to be abandoned in the lead-up to war being declared between Britain and Germany on 3 September.

More extraordinarily still, the country's greatest archaeological find to that date was made by a local amateur archaeologist, who was only there because he'd been invited by the owner of Sutton Hoo to investigate the mysterious mounds she'd been contemplating for years from her house. Basil Brown was recommended to her by Ipswich Museum on account of his familiarity with and knowledge of Suffolk soils.

Edith Pretty bought the Sutton Hoo estate in 1926 shortly after her marriage to Frank, who sadly died of stomach cancer after just eight years of marriage. Edith was active in her community, serving as a magistrate, and also supported a spiritualist church in Woodbridge, a short distance from Sutton Hoo across the River Deben. Another of Edith's interests was archaeology, inspired by her father who took his family to see Luxor and Pompeii, and who had excavated the foundations of a Cistercian abbey close to the family home.

It was Edith's sister who introduced her to spiritualism through the healer William Parish after Frank's terminal diagnosis. Spiritualism began as a social religious movement in the 19th century and continues to this day, offering 'evidence to the bereaved that man survives the change called death and ... spiritual healing to those suffering from disease' (The Spiritualist Association of Great Britain).

Because of Edith's belief in spiritualism, the story that she was motivated to excavate the mounds by a vision of a warrior standing on the largest one is popular but unsubstantiated. However, it's clear her belief gave her great comfort and could only have spurred her enthusiasm for archaeology, as both offer a bridge to the past.

Edith invited Basil Brown to Sutton Hoo in June 1938. He started his investigations straightaway, keeping a detailed diary of his work, which is as much of a treasure as all that he went on to find. The first year uncovered nothing of great note, but there was enough to warrant a second season of excavation. The following year, a discovery was made that would bring Sutton Hoo to the world's attention. His diary entry for 11 May reads: '... uncovered five rivets in position on what turned out to be the extreme prow or stern of a ship.' That ship turned out to be 27 metres long, the timbers long since rotted away, leaving its curving impression in the sand, dotted with rivets, the 'ghost' of the ship.

The archaeologists uncovered a king's burial chamber, the richest grave ever excavated in Europe, with finds of gold, garnet, silver, bronze, enamel and glass.

As soon as word of what Basil had uncovered got out, experts from the archaeological community descended on the site, taking over the dig and leaving Basil feeling somewhat sidelined. We know that on 2 July Basil went to a meeting at Woodbridge Spiritualist Church, surely on Edith's advice. We can suppose the practical autodidact that was Basil Brown was a sceptic before attending the service, but what happened to him there might well have challenged his views.

Basil walked into the church and tried hiding at the back of the congregation, but his presence was uncovered. His diary reads: 'The medium walked across the platform and said that she was coming to the gentleman in the corner … was very positive in what she said. "I see green fields … Now I see lots of sand … Now someone is holding you up in your business … ASSERT YOURSELF … go on digging and you will find what you are looking for".'

On 14 June the archaeologists uncovered a king's burial chamber, the richest grave ever excavated in Europe, with finds of gold, garnet, silver, bronze, enamel and glass, demonstrating a quality of craftsmanship never previously seen or even considered possible in objects from this period. These are thought to be the grave goods of King Rædwald, King of the East Angles until his death in around 624. The manner of his burial provided invaluable information about the lives of the Anglo-Saxons and, of course, their preparations for the afterlife.

When you visit Sutton Hoo today, particularly on a day when mist from the River Deben clings to the mounds, it's easy to imagine what the place meant to the Anglo-Saxons when they laid their dead to rest here and to sense their presence. Such a wealth of knowledge of past lives cannot help but fire the imagination.

NORTHERN ENGLAND

LYME, CHESHIRE

L yme was the family seat of the Leghs from the end of the 14th century right up to the middle of the 20th, when Richard Legh gave it to the National Trust. The first Legh of Lyme was Piers, as was the second. Sir Piers Legh II distinguished himself on the battlefields of France during the Hundred Years' War (which actually went on from 1337 to 1453 with occasional truces). The first legend of Legh relates how, when Sir Piers II fell during the Battle of Agincourt, his devoted mastiff bitch stood over and protected him until the battle's end. She returned to Lyme with her master and was immortalised not only in the stained-glass window in the Drawing Room, but also as the matriarch of the Lyme Hall Mastiffs, the pedigree largely responsible for the modern breed.

Sir Piers II and his dog were clearly devoted to each other; Sir Piers and his wife, less so. Or at least, when Sir Piers was fatally wounded seven years later at the Siege of Meaux, it was not his wife Joan who mourned him, but his mistress Blanche. This is the second legend of Legh to relate, and it's perhaps Lyme's most famous ghost story.

This is not our only story told about a Lady in White (there are 14 such apparitions matching that description to feature between the covers of this book), but she's the only one named Blanche, so her ghost would be unlikely to take on another shade. When Blanche learned of Sir Piers' death, it's said she was so stricken with grief that she died – stories vary as to whether from a broken heart or by her own hand – and her body was discovered nor far from Lyme, in a meadow that came to be known as Lady's Grave. For centuries after, witnesses have described seeing her ghost trailing the phantom funeral of her lover as it processes across the parkland of Lyme. As she was Sir Piers' mistress, it would not have been appropriate for her to be part of the mourning party and she had to grieve at a distance.

Sightings of Lyme's Lady in White were so numerous she came to be accepted as part of local folklore, but for some her presence was more troublesome. There is a building called the Cage in the park at Lyme, probably originally built as a hunting lodge and later used as staff accommodation. At the beginning of the 20th century, Joe Morten, who was employed as a shepherd on the estate, and his family were living in the Cage, but felt they had to leave as they were so discomfited by the sight of Blanche's ghost (over time, reports feature the funeral procession less and less, and the more recent accounts mention only the figure of Blanche).

Spirits besides that of the Lady in White linger at Lyme, and there have been more encounters between ghosts and staff, though none that made anyone feel they had to leave. A member of staff recalled an episode when her little boy was two and the family was living in apartments inside the house. One day, he was happy chatting away to no one in particular, as toddlers are wont to do, but when she asked who he was talking to he replied, 'To the little boy, Mummy.'

In the 18th century, Peter Legh XIII and his wife Martha had two sons, both of whom died young, one drowning in the lake in front of Lyme. Their marriage didn't survive these tragic losses and the couple separated, though it's believed Martha has returned to Lyme as the Green Lady looking for her lost sons. And perhaps one of those little boys is also here.

Lyme is a grand mansion, one with many rooms, and all the rooms that are open to the public have been expertly curated by the National Trust to show the opulent lifestyle enjoyed by the Leghs. However, there is one room that leaves some visitors cold.

The Knight's Bedroom has long had a reputation for being haunted. There was a story much told of a skeleton being discovered under the floorboards of this room during 17th-century renovations, but there has been no way of corroborating that discovery. However, what is undeniable is that, out of all of Lyme's rooms, it's the Knight's Bedroom that gives visitors pause: sensing the presence of someone who can't be seen; feeling suddenly chilled, not in a physical sense but to the point that their hairs stand on end. These people know nothing of the skeleton, as that story dropped out of circulation some time ago, but they know what they feel in this room and not in any other.

Now we continue northwards and on to the haunt of our next woman in white.

SAMLESBURY HALL, LANCASHIRE

Samlesbury Hall is a medieval manor house dating back to the 14th century and was home to the Southworth family until the 1600s. Though the Southworths moved out long ago, their link to Samlesbury Hall endures, largely due to the presence of a ghostly woman in white who has drawn the attention of paranormal investigators worldwide. Crews from the UK television show *Most Haunted* as well as America's *Ghost Hunters International* have both spent time in the hall, and many visitors come to learn about its history but also in the hope of seeing the shadow of a figure from the past step through the temporal veil into the present.

The hall's White Lady has appeared on many occasions, to visitors as well as staff. She is thought to be the ghost of Dorothy Southworth, who lived at Samlesbury in the 1500s. The Southworths were devoutly Catholic, at a time when the religious beliefs a person held could be their undoing, and so it was for Dorothy's paramour. She had fallen in love with a young man from a Protestant family. Her father refused them permission to marry, but they defied him and continued to see each other, sneaking off to spend time together on the banks of the River Ribble. During these secret assignations they were hatching a plan to elope, but word of their intentions got back to Dorothy's family, who made their own arrangements.

Under cover of darkness, thinking that would help to conceal their escape, Dorothy waited at the appointed spot, but as soon as her lover arrived, her brother leapt from his place of hiding and killed the young man along with his two companions. Dorothy witnessed the whole terrible event. She was so traumatised and beyond consolation that her family sent her away to a convent, where it's said she died of a broken heart. While her body rests elsewhere, her heart and her spirit still reside at Samlesbury, her ghost mournfully drifting through the hall.

The taint of religious intolerance marks Samlesbury Hall's history. In common with many houses of the period, the hall has several hiding places, but they weren't enough to save a Catholic priest in the 1500s, who was discovered, dragged out and decapitated on the spot. It's said that his blood left a stain that repeatedly reappeared after scrubbing, forcing a later owner to replace the floorboards. Also ingrained in the room in which the priest was slain is said to be an angry and occasionally violent ghost.

The violent factionalism of the Catholic and Protestant faiths nearly caused another Southworth to come to harm, involving accusations of witchcraft. Jane Southworth had married into the family, but to a member of the family who had abandoned the Catholic faith. In 1612, shortly after her husband died, she found herself, along with two other women, accused of witchcraft, with specific charges of child murder and cannibalism. Their accuser was a 14-year-old girl, Grace Sowerbutts, the granddaughter and niece of the other two women accused. Her incredible accusations included the murder of a one-year-old baby whose body the women had allegedly dug up, cooked and eaten, saving the fat to make a magic ointment.

Thankfully, Grace crumbled under questioning and admitted that the parish priest, who remained Catholic and disapproved of Sarah and the others' rejection of the faith, had told her to make these accusations.

The three women were acquitted but must have suffered a terrible ordeal with the threat of execution hanging over them. Not all were so fortunate, as we will see at our next destination.

PENDLE HILL, LANCASHIRE

Pendle Hill, an isolated hill in the Pennines, has drawn people to it since the earliest days of human habitation. A Bronze Age burial site has been discovered at its summit, but it's the events of the 17th century for which Pendle Hill is best known. Some of those events made positive contributions to people's lives – experiments in the field of science, revelations of a religious nature – but then there were those that took a far more sinister turn and conferred on Pendle Hill a notoriety that lives on to this day. You may find locals who are still uneasy discussing what happened here hundreds of years ago.

The spirits said to haunt Pendle Hill belong to 10 people who were sentenced to death by hanging for witchcraft. Witch trials

were conducted in England from the 15th to the 18th century and it's estimated that they resulted in the deaths of around 500 people, the great majority of whom were women. The Pendle witch trial is noteworthy not only for convicting, and executing, so many people in one set of proceedings, but also for being the best documented case of its kind, all set down in *The Wonderfull Discoverie of Witches in the Countie of Lancaster* (1613), written by the clerk to the Lancaster Assizes, Thomas Potts.

To have so many witches identified in one Lancashire village suggests either the locals were possessed of a dangerous degree of devilry, or it was all down to human folly, feuds and fanaticism.

In the 1600s, in Pendle and elsewhere, it was not unusual for peasants, usually old women, to eke out a living as herbalists, healers and soothsayers. In fact, in some places it became quite the crowded market. This appears to have been the case at Pendle, with two families led by elderly matriarchs – Elizabeth Southerns aka Demdike ('Devil woman') and Anne Chattox – who were in competition with each other. They might have carried on selling their talismans and potions, and being largely tolerated by their neighbours, but for a dispute that came to the attention of an especially zealous witch-hunter.

On 21 March 1612, Demdike's granddaughter Alizon Device stopped a pedlar, John Law, wanting to procure pins from him. Whether she was begging and refusing to pay or he didn't want to sell to her is unknown. What is known is that Law stumbled and fell shortly after this exchange – most historians suspect he suffered a stroke – and Alizon, convinced of her own powers, was so consumed with guilt that she confessed to cursing him.

Alizon was brought before the local magistrate and, on questioning, managed to implicate not only herself but her grandmother and two members of the Chattox family. Matters escalated further when a meeting was organised at Demdike's home, for which Alizon's brother stole a sheep to feed everyone. Neighbours' patience had by now been exhausted and the 'coven' was reported. So one disagreement between a pedlar and a peasant girl, for whom life would have been difficult enough, led to a deadly witch-hunt.

Those who fell under suspicion didn't exactly help themselves, with the rivalry between the families leading to accusations and counter-accusations. This was an incredibly dangerous thing to do, given the fear and hysteria generated in the community in response to the idea that powerful individuals in league with the Devil lived among them. It gave the state-appointed witch-hunters every power to persecute anyone on whom suspicion fell, and the smallest amount of 'evidence' – the presence of a birthmark, an involuntary tic, even a lazy eye – could send someone to the gallows.

It's undeniably a chilling location, one with overwhelmingly strong associations with a ruthless passage of human history.

Twelve people – including two men – were sent to the York and Lancaster assizes to stand trial, all from the area around Pendle Hill. Three women from Samlesbury (see page 96, Samlesbury Hall) were tried at the same assizes as those from Pendle Hill, in Lancaster. Demdike died in custody before she could be sentenced, one was found not guilty and the rest were sentenced to death by hanging.

While locals commemorate these tragic events – on the 400th-anniversary a statue was unveiled of one of the victims – some still fear visiting the hill at night, with reports of shadowy figures being seen darting over it. Some visitors have reported being overcome with feelings of anger, others, including members of the *Most Haunted* television crew, reported the sensation of being strangled.

It's undeniably a chilling location, one with overwhelmingly strong associations with a ruthless period of human history.

CLAIFE HEIGHTS, CUMBRIA

You may be familiar with the Scottish Munros, mountains with a height over 914 metres, but are you aware of Marilyns? These are hills with a relative height, or prominence, of more than 150 metres. Claife Heights on the west shore of Lake Windermere in Cumbria is one such example of a Marilyn but, leaving topographical punning aside, it's also home to a chilling ghost known as the Crier of Claife, the only ghost to appear on an Ordnance Survey map.

This clamorous ghost resides in a long-forgotten and wooded quarry area, and for it to become a local landmark points to its long history of haunting. Indeed, the ghost is believed to belong to a monk from Furness Abbey, which was founded in the 12th century. It was one of the most powerful Cistercian monasteries in the country until it was dissolved and destroyed in 1537 during the English Reformation. Before this calamity befell the monks at Furness Abbey, one of them was called upon by

Windermere locals to exorcise the spirit of a monk who had died, wailing in anguish, on the lakeshore. The story goes that the monk had fallen in love with a woman who rejected him, leaving the monk broken hearted and in fear for his immortal soul, having abandoned his holy vows. He died of despair and madness, his body sinking to the ground but his cries living on in the air. So unnerving were the screams that the ferrymen refused to operate the service that took people from Far Sawrey to Ferry Nab on the eastern shore. People living nearby, who needed to be able to cross Windermere, had already endured years of haunting before they finally took action – prompted by the dramatic events of one night.

The earliest account of those events was published in the Christmas Day edition of *The Kendal Mercury* in 1852, the Victorians loving a yuletide ghost story. It begins in classic fashion – 'It was a wild stormy night about Martinmas, somewhere about 330 years ago ...' – and tells how a new ferryman, sceptical of the existence of the Crier of Claife, decided to ignore both the fearful warnings of locals and the terrible weather conditions, and instead heeded the calls coming across the water, cries so piercing they could be heard through the storm. He rowed out across the water into darkness and soon disappeared from view, so no one saw what he encountered. *The Kendal Mercury* picks up the story: '... the boatman had returned alone, a sober, silent man, with terror marked in every feature of his face. He was with difficulty got to bed, and awoke next morning in a violent fever, that carried him off in a few days, but he never could be prevailed upon to say a word of what had befallen him at the Nab.' The story continues: 'These times were the days of Abbeys and Convents, and the Cistercian Monks held sway and ruled Furness Fells from the Abbey of Saint Mary in Furness, and a monk or friar used to attend the little convent on Chapel Island, half a mile north of Bowness Bay, to ease the inhabitants of the district of their sins and money .... As to the exact year in which the ceremony was performed, all is left in doubt and dimmest twilight, but there is every certainty that it was Christmas day when the monks and their attendants met the zealous inhabitants of the thinly-populated district on Chapel Island.'

The Crier of Claife was exorcised and the spirit confined to a disused quarry out of the way on the far shore. The lakeland locals were able to resume their lives free from fear of the Crier of Claife, but while the spirit might have been quietened, it appears to have not found its eternal rest. Ramblers roaming the heights have reportedly seen a shadowy figure in the woods and some have described how a hooded figure has stalked them in the vicinity of the quarry.

NUNNINGTON HALL, NORTH YORKSHIRE

The oldest surviving parts of Nunnington Hall are thought to have been built in the mid-16th century by William Parr, 1st Marquess of Northampton and brother of Catherine Parr. She was the sixth wife of Henry VIII, the one who managed to outlive him, coming last in the schoolroom mnemonic 'Divorced, Beheaded, Died, Divorced, Beheaded,

Survived'. Our tour encounters the restless spirits of numbers two (Anne Boleyn), three (Jane Seymour) and five (Catherine Howard) (see pages 85, Blickling; 34, Tower of London and 44, Hampton Court), but the ghost of Nunnington Hall is another who had dynastic struggles of her own. She is known as the Proud Lady of Nunnington and you just know, with a name such as that, hers is a tale of disastrous folly.

After the time of William Parr, who died without having any children, a woman came to live at Nunnington Hall as the then tenant's second wife, together with him and his son from his previous marriage. At first she may have tolerated the presence of the son, but after she and her husband had a son of their own, she began to treat the boy very cruelly, in classic evil stepmother style. When her husband died, she was free to openly victimise the child and she confined him to a locked room up in the attic. It's said her son was actually rather fond of his half-brother, his only playmate, and would bring him food and toys. Quite what her long-term plan for the older boy was we'll never know, as one night he managed to escape, never to be seen again.

The woman must have been overjoyed by this turn of events – he had voluntarily cleared the way for her son to inherit – but the young boy was left bereft and would spend days on end staring forlornly out of the windows and willing his brother to return. One day he leaned too far out of a window and fell to his death. His mother was inconsolable, wracked with both grief and guilt, and for the rest of her life paced through the house, lamenting her loss and her folly. After she died, the house passed to new owners and sightings began of a ghost of a woman in a silk dress, the rustling of her skirts audible, gliding through rooms and up the staircase.

We know these sightings started before the mid-1800s as the story of the Proud Lady featured in the 1866 children's book *Mia and Charlie* by Annie Keary, who grew up in the village.

In the 1930s, a French visitor was put in the Panelled Bedroom and reported seeing an apparition that came each night through the wall above her head and went out the window. In the 1950s, Nunnington Hall was given to the National Trust and reports from staff and visitors alike of inexplicable sights and sounds continued: glimpses of shadowy figures and children's whispers coming from the attic. But though the sadness of the Proud Lady's tale lingers on in some form at Nunnington Hall, this picturesque house and garden on the banks of the River Rye dispel all gloom.

TREASURER'S HOUSE, NORTH YORKSHIRE

Treasurer's House, over the road from the breathtakingly beautiful York Minster, is so called as this was where the residence of the controller of the cathedral's finances once stood. But come the Reformation, when Henry VIII assumed total control of the Church of England and its finances, York Minster's treasurer was out of a job and his house became the property of the Crown, before being passed into private ownership. The property had a succession of owners, gaining its present appearance in the 17th century when it was almost entirely rebuilt. Then in the late 19th century it was bought by a wealthy industrialist, Frank Green. While respecting its antiquity, Mr Green also wanted a comfortable house in which to entertain, so he had coal-fired central heating installed. It was Mr Green who gave the house to the National Trust, with a warning that he would come back and haunt the place if anything was done to it that was not to his liking. Naturally, the Trust has been a very careful custodian but the not infrequent wafts of cigar smoke, which vanish as quickly as they're detected, have been attributed to Mr Green's ghost periodically passing through to check up on things.

Mr Green may have been the last owner to have a psychic attachment to the place, but he wasn't the first. Strange events and inexplicable phenomena have been reported since the National Trust took over at Treasurer's House, many of them in the Tapestry Room. In this room there's a mirror, in which, if you look into it long enough, it's said the Grey Lady will appear. This takes a willing and open mind, but also in this room there have been interactions between the Grey Lady and those with no prior knowledge. On at least two separate occasions, each time to the mortification of their parents, children have broken away from a group and run over and jumped on a chair in the Tapestry Room. When they've been pulled up on their behaviour and asked why they acted in that way, the children have protested, saying they were asked to climb up on the chair so they could sit on the lady's lap.

Down in the basement, where the café now is, many visitors have enquired who owns the black cat, and is it a good idea to have an animal wandering around a kitchen? Be reassured – or perhaps not – there is no cat *living* in the basement of Treasurer's House.

Also in the basement, but in an area where visitors are unable to go, is the house's most famous haunting, even though it's only been reported by very few people and the last was over 70 years ago. But the devil's in the detail and the story just won't die, so here it is.

The first person to report strange goings-on in the cellar was a guest of Frank Green, who went down there in search of more wine. When she was barred from entry by a man in Roman soldier's uniform, she complained to her host, presumably because she wanted another drink and nobody had told her it was a fancy-dress party. It was not, and there was no man matching that description in the house. You would have noticed.

The best-known encounter was in 1953, when 18-year-old apprentice plumber Harry Martindale was repairing pipework in the cellar, the National Trust having decided to replace Mr Green's central-heating system. Intent on his work at the top of a

ladder, Harry became gradually aware of a sound, like the blast of a trumpet. It got louder and closer and louder and closer, until it sounded as though it was just the other side of the wall. Then, through that wall, marched a Roman soldier, closely followed by a horse and another 20 soldiers, two abreast. From the knees up, the soldiers looked solid and real to Harry and he observed them in detail: they looked to be in their 30s or 40s, wore green, shabby-looking uniforms, carried round shields on their left arms and daggers in their right hands. From the knees down, they were invisible.

This was too much for Harry and he fled the cellar. The warden came across him and, seeing him visibly shaken, said: 'By the look of you, you've seen the Roman soldiers.' Others were less believing, especially academics who dismissed his account because of what they thought was its inaccurate description of the soldiers. Then, in 1969, research following excavations in the city revealed that Harry's description was actually remarkably accurate, with details he could never have known; after all, the scholars of Roman history at the time didn't know them either. When the Romans returned home in the 5th century, local reserve soldiers took over military duties in the city, and this older, somewhat rag-tag bunch was what Harry had described – a kind of Dad's Army, or *exercitus patri* if you will.

Excavations also revealed that Treasurer's House was built on top of one of the major roads in Eboracum (the Roman name for York), the Via Decumana, but the level of the road was about a foot below the cellar floor, hence the missing legs and feet.

We'll come to more missing body parts shortly (see page 112, Thackray Museum of Medicine), but first we'll call on East Riddlesden Hall.

EAST RIDDLESDEN HALL, WEST YORKSHIRE

The impressive façade of East Riddlesden Hall tells you this was once the residence of the well-to-do. Much of what you see was built in the mid-17th century by a wealthy clothier, James Murgatroyd, on the site of a much older building, although he died in 1653 before all his planned renovations could be completed. It boasts not one but two rose windows, with fine panelling, decorative plasterwork and intricate woodcarvings throughout. Today it's a Grade I-listed building and considered one of Yorkshire's best examples of 17th-century vernacular architecture. It's just as well so much of the fabric of the building has been preserved, as when the hall was donated to the National Trust it had virtually no contents.

What East Riddlesden Hall did contain in abundance, however, were the spirits of people from across the building's 400-year history, whose fates would bind them forever within its walls, some more literally than others.

The hall's most famous ghost is the Grey Lady, who lived, loved and died at East Riddlesden Hall during the Tudor period. It's said that she and her lover were killed by her husband after he returned home unexpectedly and discovered their affair. While the husband was so enraged that he was driven to commit murder, his was no hot-headed crime of passion. His revenge was enacted slowly and sadistically. He starved his wife to death by imprisoning her in a room, but perhaps even worse was the fate of her lover, who was bricked up behind a wall, his screams surely audible to his lover.

Several of those who have encountered the Grey Lady have been children, who come to the hall on school trips without any prior knowledge of the place or its haunted reputation. Tour guides have been asked by their school groups about 'that lady in the corner', only to turn and find nobody there. While sightings of the Grey Lady have been so often reported that she's considered part of the building, when a visitor captured what he believed to be a spectre on film in 2016, it caused quite a stir and was picked up by a number of media outlets.

Other spirits linger at East Riddlesden Hall, the circumstances of their deaths less known, but given they're still here in some form, we can infer that they weren't ready to go. There's the ghost of a merchant, who's thought to have been murdered here. Outside there's the ghost of a woman, thought to have been thrown from her horse while she was hunting. Her body was never found and it's believed she fell into the lake where she drowned.

However, for all the sightings, there's never been a report of a menacing presence, so East Riddlesden Hall's ghosts can continue to be considered just part of the building.

THACKRAY MUSEUM OF MEDICINE, WEST YORKSHIRE

This grand and imposing Victorian building was once the Leeds Union Workhouse, built to house around 800 of the poorest citizens of Leeds. As the name implies, they were there to work and, while preferable to being out on the streets, conditions were harsh in the extreme. Victorian social welfare came with a side serving of moralising punishment, and workhouses were part correctional facilities, their architecture having a lot in common with prisons, as if their inmates needed to be shown the errors of their impoverished ways. Long hours of work would be sustained by nothing more than bread and gruel, and disease and death were not uncommon.

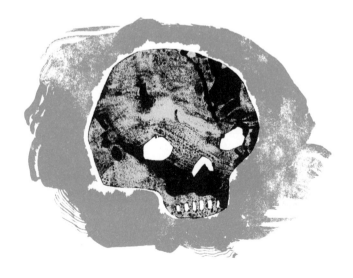

By the end of the 19th century, workhouses were, thankfully, falling out of favour – although not abolished until 1930 – and the building was in use as an infirmary. However, it was not healthcare as we know it – operations were performed without anaesthetic and survival rates were low. Now the building is a museum dedicated to the history of medicine and displays relate in graphic detail what surgical procedures used to look like. One tells the true story of eight-year-old Hannah Dyson, who had her lower leg crushed by machinery at the mill where she was working. The amputation was carried out while she was conscious and held down by the surgeon's assistants. She died three days later.

The pain, suffering and anguish of many inmates and patients are contained in these walls, leading to the building's reputation as one of Leeds' most haunted, and ghost hunts are regularly conducted here. The ghost hunters are drawn by reports of a white-coated doctor who walks the corridors, doing his rounds for eternity; a 19th-century woman known as the Grey Lady; or of people being grabbed by unseen hands, hearing disembodied footsteps, whispers and crying, knocking and banging.

As well as this host of ghosts, the Thackray Museum of Medicine was until 2015 home to the Yorkshire Witch – or at least the skull and other bones belonging to the woman named as and sentenced to death for being a witch. (Her skeletal remains and death mask now belong to Leeds University Medical School.) Mary Bateman was a career criminal, who along with burglary dabbled in a spot of fortune-telling and developed a reputation as a 'wise woman'. In 1806 she joined a sect and created a hoax known as the Prophet Hen of Leeds, in which a hen laid eggs that came out with miraculous messages written on them, messages that warned of the end of days. She would charge members of the public a penny a time to see them. It may come as no surprise that Bateman wrote these messages herself and reinserted the prophetic eggs into the hen, for whom it was most certainly a surprise.

Bateman's crimes worsened and she was found guilty of poisoning a woman whom she was fraudulently, and fatally, medicating with potions to treat an illness. Bateman was hanged in 1809 and her body was taken to Leeds General Infirmary, where it was displayed to the public for thruppence a gawk. More macabre still, following her ticketed dissection that was spread over three days such was the demand from members of the public, strips of her skin were tanned into leather and sold as magic charms to ward off evil spirits.

Fortunately, not many of the spirits in this book could be described as evil, so we'll take no such precautions and move on to our next property.

BAMBURGH CASTLE, NORTHUMBERLAND

Bamburgh Castle preserves many centuries of history, from its foundation as a Celtic fort in the 5th century to its conversion to a stately home by Victorian industrialist William Armstrong. It also came under attack from Viking marauders in the 10th century and was the first castle to fall to gunpowder during the War of the Roses.

To look at Bamburgh's arrestingly beautiful silhouette commanding views over the Northumberland coast, it seems more fairy tale than ghost story, but that is the curiosity of castles, that they can conjure up so much death but also romance at the same time. It's entirely possible for a place to be the scene of many contrasting stories, and at Bamburgh, as with so many castles, you can have the turreted towers for princesses to gaze forlornly from, and precarious battlements from which unfortunates plummet to their deaths. So it's entirely fitting that Bamburgh's most famous ghost has tragedy and romance in abundance.

She is the Pink Lady, who was a Northumbrian princess and said to have been stunningly beautiful. Whether she was or not is not important; what's key to this story is that she fell in love with a man of whom her father did not approve. In other stories with a similar set-up, the overbearing and power-corrupted parent had the unsuitable subject of their offspring's affection killed, but this was apparently a kindlier king and he merely had him exiled for seven years, hoping some time apart would cool their ardour. But her love was so profound – or the opportunities to meet new boys in medieval Northumbria so limited – that she continued to pine.

Six years or more passed and the princess was still terribly depressed. The king, at a loss to know what to do with his lovesick daughter, thought the best course of action would be to tell her that her sweetheart had married someone else, while at the same time giving her a pretty pink dress to cheer her up. She received the news and the dress, took herself up to her chamber to put it on, and then climbed the stairs to the top of the castle's highest battlements and threw herself off.

With the sense of timing reserved for only the best romantic heroes, her lover returned a short time later, unmarried and desperate to be reunited. His heart was broken but his part in the story ends there. The princess, however, every seven years returns to Bamburgh, dressed in her pink shroud. She has been seen making her way along the castle's corridors and then outside, where she takes the path down to the beach and takes up her sad vigil, watching and waiting for her true love's return.

While the Pink Lady is certainly Bamburgh's most famous ghost, she is not the only one. There have been reports of apparitions in the forms of knights and soldiers, who would have made up many of the casualties in defence of the castle. More easily identified is the ghost of Dr John Sharp, whose portrait hangs prominently in the King's Hall. This was a man who invested so much of his energy in Bamburgh that it's no surprise to people familiar with his story that he maintains a presence here in the afterlife.

Dr Sharp was an archdeacon and philanthropist who put a huge amount of his time and money into charitable causes in the area. Before the castle was bought by William Armstrong and converted into a stately home, a board of trustees led by Dr Sharp was responsible for the castle, renovating it and saving it from ruin but also establishing a hospital on the site, a godsend for locals and shipwreck victims alike, as the remoteness of the area did nothing for survival rates. Dr Sharp's ghost has been seen by staff and members of the Armstrong family who still live in part of the castle, and is regularly reported by visitors who recognise him from his portrait.

Bookending Bamburgh's ghosts is another colourful spirit who goes by the name of Green Jane. She and, more tragically still, her baby fell to their deaths from the top of Miller's Nick. This was the name given to the narrow and steep way up and through the castle's walls to the mill where the local community brought their grain for grinding. Jane had been told by her family to go up to the castle and beg for food, her baby clutched to her chest. The castle guards were unsympathetic and turned her away. Whether they did so forcefully, causing her to stumble, or she did so out of hunger-induced weakness isn't known, but down she and her bundle fell. The sightings that have been reported are the distressing echoes of this very scene: a woman in green carrying something under her cloak is seen on the stone staircase; she staggers and cries out before tumbling down the narrow steps; by the time those who have rushed to help her arrive, she is nowhere to be seen. When the castle is quiet and all but empty, people have also reported hearing the cries of a baby.

CHILLINGHAM CASTLE, NORTHUMBERLAND

Given Chillingham Castle was the scene of years of battling and bloodshed – some of it in conflict, much more of it, as we shall see, in the castle's torture chamber – it's perhaps unsurprising that this castle is said to be one of the most haunted in all of Britain. Originally a monastery founded in the 12th century, by 1298 it was a castle receiving royalty, when Edward I stopped off on his way to fight William Wallace's rebels at the Battle of Falkirk in the First War of Scottish Independence. For much of its history it was home to the Grey family, who gained distinction through service to the Crown and were rewarded with titles. They were further immortalised by many mentions in Shakespeare's history plays and by Earl Grey tea. But the family's loyalties at times served them less well, such as during the 15th-century Wars of the Roses when they backed the Yorkists, and had no fewer than eight members of the family executed at Chillingham Castle. These were performative, make-an-example-of executions, in which the unfortunates were hanged, drawn and quartered, their heads finally removed and impaled on spikes for all to see.

However, these notables were just a few among the many who met their grisly ends here; some time before these executions Chillingham Castle had gained a reputation for sadistic punishment. This was all the work of its jailer, interrogator and torturer, a man named John 'Dragfoot' Sage, also known as the Butcher of the Scots. It's thought he was employed by Edward I between 1296 and 1299 and tasked with torturing Scottish prisoners to get them to reveal the whereabouts of William Wallace. It's a task he clearly relished, making and improvising several terrifying devices.

The Torture Chamber at Chillingham Castle is open to the public today and displays examples of these horrifying artefacts. It's not the original torture chamber, which is in a sealed-off vault below the castle, closed to the public after a seance produced terrifying results. Sage's devices included the trademark stretching rack, iron maiden, chair of nails and pear of anguish (an expanding metal pear inserted into the body's orifices) but also one of his own invention – a barrel filled with nails into which the victim was placed before it was rolled away, skinning that person alive. But his preferred method of torture was to place his victim in a person-shaped cage and suspend them over a fire. Such was this man's reputation for evil, it was said he wore a hood of past victims' blackened skin while he worked.

William Wallace was finally located and Edward met him and his forces at the Battle of Falkirk, crushing the Scottish rebellion, for a while at least. On his return, Edward gave the order to have the prisoners released. Sage followed this order but not before lighting an enormous bonfire in the castle courtyard. The prisoners were turned out of the castle but driven onto the pyre. More sadistic still, Sage rounded up the children of the prisoners into the Edward I Room that overlooked the courtyard and made them watch, before they were butchered by Sage with a small axe still on display at the castle.

Cries were heard coming from a spot in the three-metre-thick wall followed by a bright blue light, out of which guests saw a boy dressed in blue emerge.

Of the many ghosts believed to haunt Chillingham Castle, Sage's victims unsurprisingly make up the majority. Disembodied screams of terror and pain are sometimes heard, as well as the popping sound of bones being dislodged on the rack. In the Edward 1 Room, also known as the Killing Room, visitors have reported feeling overcome by sadness and some have been overwhelmed by what they've described as the smell of human blood. Perhaps fittingly, one of Chillingham's ghosts is thought

to belong to the Butcher himself, who met his own end in a suitably agonising fashion.

He was found to have murdered a clan chief's daughter with whom he was having an affair. Sage's usefulness to Edward was at an end, so to avoid trouble with the locals he handed Sage over to them and they strung him up, using a short rope that choked him slowly to death rather than swiftly breaking his neck. His body was mutilated – the villagers cutting off the nose, testicles and toes to take as souvenirs – before it was thrown into a cesspit. Sage's ghost is said to haunt the scene of his many crimes, some say in search of his missing body parts.

While Sage is an undeniably evil presence in Chillingham Castle, best left confined to his sealed-off torture chamber, there is another famous ghost who goes by the name of the Blue Boy who haunts above stairs, in the Pink Room. Cries were heard coming from a spot in the three-metre-thick wall followed by a bright blue light, out of which guests saw a boy dressed in blue emerge. Subsequently, during renovation work, behind that wall were discovered the bones of a child, with decaying fragments of blue cloth still clinging to them. The body was given a proper burial and for a time the sightings stopped, but when the current owners started letting out the room, some guests complained of a flash of blue light shooting out of the wall at night. While it might be logical to suppose an electrical fault of some kind, there is no wiring in that section of wall.

Back below stairs, but stopping short of Sage's torture chamber, in the Inner Pantry is the ghost of a woman in white. This is the room in which the family silver was kept under lock and key with a footman to guard it. The story goes that the footman was woken one night by a pale and frail woman asking for water. At first, assuming it was one of the castle's guests who'd become thirsty in the night, he went to get the water. But then he remembered he was locked in and no guest could possibly have entered. She promptly vanished but she is still seen on occasion, still asking for water, with some attributing her thirst to poisoning.

Chillingham Castle contains almost too many spirits to recount – Lady Leonora who was living at the castle in the 1920s wrote in her diary: 'I had no idea there could be so many apparitions living under one roof' – but the last to note is that of Lady Mary Berkeley. She was married to Lord Grey and lived at Chillingham at the end of the 17th century. She and her baby were abandoned by Lord Grey, who ran off with Lady Mary's much-younger sister, Henrietta. Mary's rustling skirts have been heard as she eternally paces about the castle waiting for her husband's return.

We will shortly return to the misery of having a good-for-nothing husband (see page 125, Gibside), but first we shall go to Seaton Delaval Hall. However – spoiler alert – men don't come off very well in those stories, either.

SEATON DELAVAL HALL, NORTHUMBERLAND

The Delavals were an extraordinary family, whose rise and fall were completed in the space of a hundred years. They earned a reputation for eccentricity and extravagance in equal measure, contributing more than their share of scandal for the entertainment of 18th-century English society. Sir Francis Delaval gained perhaps greatest notoriety, with one story relating how he took a bet with a friend that he couldn't build a house for his mistress in one day. The family having wealth enough from their collieries and glass works and Sir Francis being fool enough to accept such a wager, building began under cover of darkness and Starlight Castle folly was completed in nearby Seaton Sluice the following day. With the exploits of some family members being mythologised in their lifetimes, it's little wonder their reputations have followed them into the afterlife. Although, as is often the case with gossip, there is more than one version of the tale.

A White Lady is said to haunt Seaton Delaval, keeping watch from a first-floor window on the north front of the house, waiting for her love to return. One account goes that she was in love with the dashing young heir of Seaton Delaval and, while she was accepted to be beautiful, Lord Delaval did not consider her worthy of his son, as he was the only male heir. In order to thwart the match, he gave orders for his son to join his regiment in Lincolnshire and not to return until he was sent for, hoping that some time apart would cool their ardour. After a few weeks, news reached Seaton Delaval that the young man had fallen dangerously ill. Lord Delaval sent a party to bring his son back home, but they arrived too late. The last male heir had died. The beautiful woman died of a broken heart and the distraught Lord Delaval built an elaborate mausoleum in his son's memory.

So goes one version, but there is another that shares some of the same details but gives another reason for the heir's premature demise.

John Delaval was the only son of Sir John Hussey Delaval and Susanna Robinson. He was also the nephew of the rake and the roué that was Sir Francis Delaval. Sir John was determined that his only son shouldn't follow the example of his wayward uncle and imposed upon him a closely regulated education. The young John, known as Jack, was painted as a 14-year-old, and the portrait depicts him as outdoorsy and energetic, whereas in truth he was a rather weak and sickly boy. Despite his strict upbringing and limited vigour – or perhaps because of them – Jack had a penchant for molesting servant girls. Like the young heir of the previous version, Jack died away from Seaton Delaval aged just 19 in July 1775. But, very unlike the romantic hero of that version, Jack was away visiting some springs in Bristol to cure an illness when he tried to force himself on a maid, who delivered a blow to his crotch so forcefully that it was enough to kill him.

Jack's obituary in the *Morning Post* ran: 'On Friday last died at Bristol, in the twentieth year of his age, after a severe illness of several months' continuance, which he bore with a truly Christian patience, John Delaval, Esq. son of Sir John Hussey Delaval, Bart. whose death is grievously lamented by his most afflicted parents, and by all who had the happiness of being acquainted with him. His manners were so pure, unaffected, and amiable, and his behaviour so engaging and irresistible, that he captured the affections, and was the delight of all that knew him.' And so on and so forth. While these notices are expected to do honour to the deceased, this encomium is so at odds with the boy's reputation and lays it on so thickly as to arouse suspicion.

And finally, just like the previous version of this story, a mausoleum *was* built to commemorate the passing of the last male heir, although it remained empty.

We've seen the tradition of a haunting arising from any number of historical contexts, but this may be the only ghost story that serves as a romantic distraction from the embarrassing truth.

GIBSIDE, TYNE AND WEAR

G ibside Hall is a literal shell of its former glorious self, though it's set in one of the finest surviving examples of 18th-century landscape design. Inside this romantic ruin is rumoured to dwell the ghost of Mary Eleanor Bowes, also known as the Unhappy Countess. While marriage can enrich the individuals involved, marry unwisely and it could lead to a lifetime – or even longer – of regret.

Gibside was once the lavish country home of the Bowes, a family made immensely wealthy through judicious marriages that led to the acquisition and combining of estates, some of which were richly veined with coal. When George Bowes inherited the family estates in 1722, his wealth and influence were almost immeasurable, as head of a coal cartel and uncontested in his constituency's elections. When he and his second wife had an only child, Mary Eleanor, he was reminded of the importance of a good marriage and the need to be vigilant against those who would pursue his daughter for the family wealth only.

George died in 1760 when Mary was just 11 years old, leaving her a vast fortune – estimated at between £600,000 and £1,000,000 in Georgian money – and making her the wealthiest heiress in Britain, perhaps in Europe. Mary's first marriage at 18 seems to have been a sound one, at least in terms of her husband's intentions and interest in the Bowes family fortune. John Lyon was an earl, the 9th Earl of Strathmore and Kinghorne, so Mary became a countess and the couple took the combined name Bowes-Lyon in accordance with a provision in her father's will. However, in 1776, after nine years of marriage, John died of tuberculosis, leaving Mary an incredibly wealthy widow.

Shortly after her husband's death, Mary was planning a second marriage, to her lover George Gray, but she had learned, perhaps from her father, to be cautious in terms of protecting her wealth and was in the process of drawing up a prenuptial agreement. This is when she tragically fell under the spell of Andrew Robinson Stoney, a handsome but heartless social climber and sociopath. So underhandedly ambitious was this man that he hatched a plan that would trick the countess into marrying him.

Having made his advances towards Mary, Stoney continued laying his trap by engaging in a battle of letters with the editor of the *Morning Post*, who had been publishing scurrilous (although certainly true) stories about the countess's extra-marital affairs (mostly fed to him by Stoney). Stoney's public defence of her reputation culminated in his challenging the editor to a duel. He then enlisted the help of a surgeon with whom he'd done military service. When Stoney and the editor met to duel to the death (which they both knew was going to look like Stoney's), his surgeon friend was there to confirm that he was almost certainly going to die from his wounds. At this moment of high drama, Stoney asked the countess to marry him. Perhaps taken in by the romance, and completely missing the deceit, she agreed.

Stoney of course made a miraculous recovery, as swiftly followed by a devastating discovery: the countess had drawn up contracts that prevented her husband from exploiting her wealth. Stoney subjected his wife to eight years of physical and mental abuse. The countess endured beatings, starvation, imprisonment and, in eventual divorce proceedings, she alleged that on one occasion her husband gagged and bound her and carried her around on horseback in the depths of an unusually cold winter.

The countess did eventually manage to escape her husband and secure a divorce, but at great cost to her health and reputation. The divorce was the subject of huge public attention and scrutiny, and sensationalised reports of the case filled the newspapers, in which she was given the title of the Unhappy Countess.

That Mary endured such torment at Gibside has led some to suppose that the ghostly figure of a woman in white, who is sometimes glimpsed near the Orangery, is that of the Unhappy

Countess. As ethereal is the organ music that has been heard emanating from the locked chapel, and the sudden and intense scent of a woman's perfume that has been caught on the air inside the ruined hall.

LUMLEY CASTLE, COUNTY DURHAM

The Lumleys have a history here dating back to the 14th century and, though Lumley Castle is now a luxury hotel conveniently located next to Durham County Cricket Ground, some would say a Lumley is still in residence.

It was Sir Ralph Lumley who first had the idea of constructing a castle in Chester-le-Street just outside Durham, on the site of the family manor house. That was in 1389. The castle became very quickly associated with violent and untimely deaths, when in 1400 Sir Ralph became involved in a plot to overthrow Henry IV and was executed.

Records state Sir Ralph was married to Eleanor Neville, who was the daughter of his guardian. However, as we know, castles must have their share of tragedy and romance, and there is a tale called 'The Lily of Lumley' in which Sir Ralph had a previous wife, who nurtured what were then regarded as heretical beliefs but whom he loved in defiance of the convention of the times. It's said that Lily was thrown down a well in the castle grounds by two priests for rejecting the Catholic faith; they subsequently covered their crime by telling Sir Ralph that she had left him to become a nun. But Lily never left Lumley, and her ghost on occasion rises up from the well and haunts the castle.

Now that the castle is a hotel and many people pass through its doors, reports of paranormal activity are numerous. Some have claimed to see apparitions, most commonly a figure in a long white dress in the Great Hall, or to hear unexplained noises echoing through the halls. Others have reported feeling a sense of unease or cold spots in certain parts of the castle.

Some of these accounts have been widely reported, as several visiting cricketers claim to have experienced peculiar goings-on at the hotel. The online media outlets of India, Australia and other cricketing nations have eagerly picked up and run with the stories, as the idea of these people being scared out of their wits and out of their rooms seems to offer a new spin (pun intended) on the macho image of the international sportsman.

When the West Indies visited in 2000, captain Jimmy Adams and two others checked out on the first night, so unsettled were

they. Then in 2002, Indian captain Sourav Ganguly claimed to have experienced paranormal activity, after which he refused to stay at Lumley Castle. In 2005, Australia and England met at the county ground for a day-night match. The visitors stayed at Lumley Castle but some had a less comfortable night's sleep than others. Shane Watson was so spooked by something he'd seen or heard in his room that he decided he'd rather sleep on the floor of teammate Brett Lee's room. Apparently this got back to England's fast bowler Darren Gough, who couldn't resist teasing Watson by offering, 'Don't worry, you can sleep in my room tonight,' and, while doing his best impression of a ghost, suggesting that Watson could only play with the lights on.

It should be stressed that, judging by the number of positive reviews the hotel has, Lily's exploits at the castle do nothing to trouble the vast majority of guests. Indeed the hotel actively encourages engagement with Lily's story and plays host to an escape-room event that has ghosts and curses as its themes.

However, if you go to Lumley Castle looking for Lily, don't be surprised if you encounter the shade of another. With this many years of history, involvement in civil wars and dungeons to boot, the walls of Lumley Castle are said to contain other souls in limbo, but their stories are unlikely to be as romantic, or marketable. Down in the dungeons is the Black Knight, who some think was a casualty of one of the many battles that took place in and around the castle walls, and who others think is a captured soldier thrown in here and forgotten about. In the chapel, an apparition of a person in 17th-century clothing has been reported, believed by some to be a Catholic sympathiser, frozen in a time when it was the Protestants who were throwing people down wells.

WALES

LLANCAIACH FAWR MANOR, CAERPHILLY

And now we come to South Wales and what is said to be one of Britain's most supernaturally active buildings. Llancaiach Fawr is just 40 minutes by car from Cardiff, but as you enter this restored Tudor manor house it's a journey that takes you back nearly 400 years. The interiors, the furnishings and the costumed interpreters are all set to the year 1645, when the manor's owner, Colonel Edward Pritchard, was embroiled in the ructions of the Civil War. Everything is carefully curated to be as historically accurate as possible and, if not original, furnishings are faithful reproductions. What is original to the house, but may not always keep to the script, are the ghosts that have made regular appearances to staff and visitors alike.

The colonel himself, in the most authentically Tudor costume of them all, has been seen in the Great Hall and his footsteps heard pacing back and forth in that room. When repeated attempts to replaster the kitchen ceiling directly below the Great Hall were made during restoration work, the experts were confounded. They could only conclude that movement above was causing the plaster to fail, which in an unoccupied house should not have been possible; it so happened the problematic patch of plaster was directly under the reputed path of Pritchard's pacing.

Below stairs too there have been supernatural stirrings. Mattie was the housekeeper here and insists on keeping house even after her death, some say in a fire that engulfed the building. Her

ghost has been seen contentedly baking bread in the kitchen on numerous occasions, but a visit to her bedroom on the upper floor is a far more desolate experience. Many have been overcome with sadness and despair on entering the room, including the captain of the South Africa under-21 rugby team, who is said to have spontaneously and inexplicably broken down in floods of tears while he stood in Mattie's bedroom.

There are also the ghosts of children who haunt the manor, with two who play on the grand staircase, appearing and then as quickly disappearing, their giggles lingering as they take delight in the fear and confusion they induce in visitors. The costumed female guides are apparently also fair game, as aprons have been known to mysteriously untie themselves and fall to the floor.

Perhaps most unnerving of all the manor's phenomena are the disembodied voices that sometimes fill the air but always seem to be coming from the next room. Sure enough, when you enter that room, there is no one to be seen but the voices can still be heard, coming from next door. The manor's antiquity has made it a popular filming location and its reputation for being one of the most haunted houses in Britain has attracted much media attention over the years. One day a film crew came and spent many hours inside the house. It seemed they must have recorded enough for a long television piece, but staff were disappointed that only a very short segment was included in the programme. When they contacted the production company to ask why so much had been cut, they were told that much of what had been filmed was unusable due to off-camera noises from an unknown and unseen source. Perhaps the ghosts too were disappointed to be denied their 15 minutes of fame.

NEWTON HOUSE, CARMARTHENSHIRE

Continuing on over the Bannau Brycheiniog (Brecon Beacons) we come to Carmarthenshire. Wales is renowned for its castles – it has over 600, more castles per square mile than any other country in Europe. More survive in ruins than intact and Dinefwr Castle – in the grounds of which Newton House is situated – is one such ghost of a castle.

Built in the 12th century for Lord Rhys, Prince of Wales, it fell into English hands by the end of the following century and gradually into ruin. Its keep, however, was kept on and adapted for use as a summer house, to be enjoyed by the residents of Newton House, which was built in 1660 by Edward Rice (an anglicisation of the name Rhys) on the site of a medieval mansion in the castle grounds. Newton House is emphatically Victorian Gothic on the outside, with turrets at each corner, their steep-sided slate roofs thrusting upwards to give this originally Jacobean house the appearance of an even taller, grander building.

Newton House and its estate sit on so many layers of occupation, have witnessed so much human history and been the scene of so many events, both bloody and benign, it's not surprising that it claims to have a resident ghost or two.

There have been many reports of paranormal activity from both staff and visitors, and it seems this may be nothing new. The house underwent extensive renovation after it came into the care of the National Trust in 1990, and in the course of this restoration some intriguing discoveries were made. A number of objects were found under the floorboards, their deliberate placement suggesting measures to ward off evil spirits and protect the household from witchcraft and supernatural forces.

Perhaps the most intriguing find was the desiccated body of a cat. This was not some unfortunate feline who crawled into a crevice on the trail of mice, but a cat clearly already departed when it was wrapped in a woven reed mat and placed under the floorboards on a slate near a front-facing window. This discovery is discussed in the book *Magical House Protection: The Archaeology of Counter-Witchcraft* by Brian Hoggard as something that was not uncommon practice: 'Cats concealed in this way were part of the supernatural armoury which people deployed in response to fear of witchcraft and other sources of harm.'

Another find at Newton House is mentioned in the same book, a bent nail driven through part of an animal's backbone. Again, in Hoggard's view, this is unlikely to be anything other than a very deliberately arranged object, the bone acting as a lure while iron nails were believed to give protection against witchcraft, especially when bent.

If these objects were placed to ward off spirits, it would appear they're not proving terribly effective, judging by the number of phantoms and unfathomable phenomena that have been and continue to be reported at Newton House. There have been sightings of the ghost of an old woman on the stairs, dressed in black and cloaked in an atmosphere of dread and despair. Below stairs, the servants' basement is considered a particular centre of paranormal activity. There have been numerous reports of mysterious apparitions and sensations.

What is believed to be the ghost of Walter the butler is seen the most often, and smelt too, tobacco smoke being suddenly and unmistakeably detectable.

Once a place gains a reputation for paranormal activity, there can be a tendency for imagination to take over. For example, the story most often told about ghosts at Newton House is that of a lady in white, believed to be the spirit of Lady Elinor Cavendish, a relation of the lady of the house in the 1720s. The story goes that she rejected a suitor and fled to Newton House to take refuge with her family, but was murdered in a second-floor room. As well as sightings of her ghost, there have been reports of people claiming to have felt invisible hands closing around their throats when they've been in or near that room. Investigations have failed to produce any evidence of the existence of a Lady Elinor or of a murder in the house. If a person of rank had been murdered, there would almost certainly be a record of it. It's now thought that the story originated with a medium who visited the house and it has gained popularity in the retelling.

A number of objects were found under the floorboards, their deliberate placement suggesting measures to ward off evil spirits.

Contrast this with the sightings that have been reported by staff and visitors of a boy in blue, who is seen to manifest on the stairs and in other places in the house. The interesting thing about this sighting is that it isn't documented, hasn't grown into a story, but reports continue from visitors about the ghost of child, often dressed in blue, following them or standing near them.

Ghosts and stories alike can materialise out of thin air; working out what is real and what is imagined is just part of our fascination with the paranormal.

LLANERCHAERON, CEREDIGION

Onwards and westwards we go, into an area that abounds in traditions and customs arising from inexplicable phenomena, such that they were compiled into a tome entitled *Folk-Lore of West and Mid-Wales* by Jonathan Ceredig Davies. This work of 1911 details customs related to love, weddings and funerals, and stories of fairies, mermaids, witches, ghosts and death portents. There has long been a sense in this part of the world of something 'other' that exists between worlds seen and unseen – be that insubstantial figures in the shadows between the light and the dark, phantom funerals or a lost world between the land and the sea.

At Llanerchaeron, a National Trust Georgian villa and estate, visitors do not often report actually seeing a ghost, but frequently describe a feeling of people unseen being present. The house is the design of John Nash – famous for Buckingham Palace, Marble Arch, the Royal Pavilion in Brighton and many more besides – and is the most complete example of his early work. But it would seem Llanerchaeron retains more than historic architecture. The house would have been at the centre of a busy estate that was designed to be as self-sufficient as possible, and many of these sensations of a presence detected, but not seen, have been reported 'below stairs'.

A number of visitors have said that they felt the presence of a man in the housekeeper's room. One day, a staff member was working in that room when the door slammed shut unexpectedly and wouldn't open again, despite having no lock. However, it was easily opened from the outside by someone passing by who heard cries for help.

There have also been reports of cooking smells emanating from the kitchens, when no such thing was going on. Volunteers, staff and visitors have noticed the smell of cooked meat, particularly fried sausages and bacon, a smell not easily mistaken. It seems to be stronger in one particular spot by the end of the small table in the window and tends to be observed when activities are taking place in the kitchens, leading some to speculate that it's the spirit of the cook being stirred, unimpressed at the way her kitchens have been overrun.

The smell of smoke, but the sort that emanates from a pipe, has been detected in the servants' corridor. Some say this is a telltale trace of the last owner of Llanerchaeron, Mr Ponsonby Lewes, who inherited the house in 1940. During his later years, Ponsonby Lewes spent a lot of time in the kitchen, reportedly rapping his walking stick against the dresser cupboard when he wanted his housekeeper's attention. It's said that the rapping could still be heard long after his death, a percussive accompaniment to his pipe smoke.

There was no phantom funeral portending Ponsonby Lewes's end, as these phenomena have been reported less and less over

the century since the publication of *Folk-Lore of West and Mid-Wales*. This book did include, however, a report of one of these phantom funerals, known in Ceredigion as *toili*. John Jones was walking along the road one evening from Derwen Gam to his home in Coed y Brenin, when he suddenly found himself part of a ghostly funeral procession and nearly passed out in fright. He managed to escape into a field, and might have tried to put the terrifying ordeal from his mind but for the fact that a few weeks later he observed once again the funeral procession taking place along the exact same route.

In the same book there is mention of an underwater realm, a Welsh Atlantis lying beneath the waters of Cardigan Bay. Described in local folklore as the home of the fairy people, the Tylwyth Teg, this story might be dismissed by some as a fanciful tale and nothing more. But a discovery made in the Bodleian

Library in 2022 gave credence to this idea of the Gwerddonau Llion, or the 'Green Islands of the Ocean'. In the Bodleian's collection is a medieval map known as the Gough Map dating to approximately 1360. While carrying out research work on the map, academics noticed two islands clearly marked in Cardigan Bay that have since disappeared from view. So maybe there are some things preserved in folklore that can't be seen but may still be believed?

PLAS NEWYDD, DENBIGHSHIRE

Not the Plas Newydd looked after by the National Trust on the banks of the Menai Strait but another 'New House', as that is how Plas Newydd translates in Welsh. This Plas Newydd was the home of the Ladies of Llangollen, Lady Eleanor Butler and Sarah Ponsonby, who ran away together leaving behind the aristocratic circles they'd been born into in Ireland.

The two women lived here together for 50 years, turning the cottage into their 'new house', a Gothic fantasy of stained-glass windows, ornate wood carvings, a 'ruined' archway and rustic bridges. They invested so much of themselves in the transformation of their home, it's hardly surprising that their presence is still strongly felt.

Their relationship and decision to spurn conventional marriages caused a great deal of curiosity, but what they built together at Plas Newydd and the many distinguished visitors they received here – Wordsworth, Shelley, Byron, the Duke of Wellington to name a few – led to fame rather than scandal.

Their fame lived on after their deaths, which happened within two years of each other, though Sarah was 16 years younger than Eleanor. In 1934, the author Mary Gordon visited Plas Newydd and claimed to have seen the ghosts of the two women, an encounter she wrote about in her book *Chase of the Wild Goose*. Gordon writes that she not only saw the ladies in the garden in their 18th-century attire – well-known from a number of portraits that were made of them – but that they invited her to come back to speak with them later that night. Gordon broke into the library and the three conversed apparently until sunrise.

> *Their spirits live on at Plas Newydd and beyond, reminding us of the importance of being free to love whomsoever we choose.*

After the Ladies of Llangollen, Plas Newydd was for a time the home of General John Yorke, whose spirit is also said to linger on, although in a rather more stentorious fashion. His spirit seems less interested in conversing with visitors and instead communicates through loud and unexplained bangs.

The numerous sightings of these ghosts, as well as others at the property, have brought many people out in pursuit of a paranormal encounter at Plas Newydd. In 2008, an episode of *Most Haunted* was filmed at the house, with four separate entities being detected: the spirits of the Ladies of Llangollen, which were experienced as benevolent and lavender-scented (lavender being a symbol of sapphic love); an angry military man, whose presence was accompanied by feelings of breathlessness and chest pains; and a young boy who had apparently suffered a fatal blow to the head. This last ghost is thought to be that of a stable lad who died after being kicked by one of the horses.

For all the paranormal activity, Plas Newydd remains a tranquil place, evocative of the idyll that Eleanor and Sarah created so that they could live the lifestyle considered so alternative for the times, and for a long time thereafter. Their spirits live on at Plas Newydd and beyond, reminding us of the importance of being free to love whomsoever we choose. Or as Wordsworth put it in his sonnet titled 'To the Lady E.B. and the Hon. Miss P.': 'Sisters in love, a love allowed to climb, / Even on this earth, above the reach of Time!'

BEAUMARIS, ANGLESEY

Across the Menai Strait is the Isle of Anglesey, and the town of Beaumaris ('beautiful marshes'). The town has two haunted fortresses, one built to keep people out, the other to keep people in. The first is Beaumaris Castle. Of the 600 and more castles in Wales, this is one of the few to avoid total ruination, but if its outline has anything in common with those castles that haven't survived so well, it's because it was never finished. Edward I had already fortified much of North Wales and built the great castles of Conwy, Caernarfon and Harlech. Beaumaris was to be the castle to beat them all, but by 1296 finances were running out and trouble in Scotland directed Edward's attention there.

The many reports of paranormal activity at Beaumaris Castle suggest souls with unfinished business, whether these are the ghosts of soldiers who fought to the death or labourers who were worked to death. The sound of heavy but invisible footsteps is frequently heard by visitors, who also report the feeling of being followed. And the castle's chapel, which like all such places of prayer maintains a reverential hush and an atmosphere of sombre silence, has been known to suddenly fill with the chanting of long-defunct monks.

Beaumaris Castle to some is undeniably haunted but, unlike other places we've visited within these pages, it's not home to the ghosts of people who can be identified. Perhaps because of the sheer scale of this building, employing over 2,000 workers to build it, it's more like a small city of souls who populate and permeate the place with feelings of unease.

On a much smaller scale is the town's other fortified building, Beaumaris Gaol. This was built in 1829 to house no more than 30 prisoners at a time. Just as now, some prisoners' crimes were so grievous their sentences were long and for life; unlike our modern-day justice system, some inmates' sentences were short and for death.

The castle's chapel, which maintains a reverential hush and an atmosphere of sombre silence, has been known to suddenly fill with the chanting of long-defunct monks.

Those spared execution might have at times wished for it, judging by the whipping room, solitary confinement cells and treadmill that prisoners would be lashed to. These are all on display at Beaumaris Gaol, now a successful tourist attraction, along with the gibbet from which two men are known to have hung.

One was William Griffith, who was sentenced to death in 1830 for the attempted murder of his ex-wife. The other was Richard Rowlands in 1862, for the murder of his father-in-law. He pleaded his innocence to the very end and legend has it that he placed a curse on the jail, specifically the church clock, saying that if he were innocent the clock would never show the correct time. Despite frequent adjustment, it never has.

For all the torment and misery experienced in this place, it would be odd if a lingering sense of sadness or unease was not experienced here. Certainly there have been many reports of ghostly murmurings, people being pulled by unseen hands, a dark energy that is concentrated around the condemned cells and a general feeling of despair, but the ghost that keeps the most regular routine of haunting is, appropriately, that of a jailer. There have been numerous and consistent reports of the same paranormal events: keys heard clanking on the metal handrail as some unseen person makes their way down the central staircase; the disembodied sounds of knocking on doors and of feet shuffling outside a cell; even a ghostly but nonchalant whistling, as the phantom jailer does his rounds of the prison.

NORTHERN IRELAND

BALLYGALLY CASTLE, COUNTY ANTRIM

This 17th-century castle has many of the features of a fortress – 1.5-metre-thick walls and loopholes for muskets – but sitting as prettily as it does, looking out over Ballygally Bay, it's difficult to imagine it as the scene of much marauding. Built in the Scottish baronial style by James Shaw in 1625, it did withstand multiple attacks during the Great Rebellion of 1641. Thereafter, it led a quieter life as the Shaw family home until the early 1800s, when financial difficulties forced its sale. When it was bought by a textile millionaire in the 1950s, its picture-postcard appearance and position on the coast made it ripe for development into a hotel, which it is to this day. While the castle has over 50 comfortable and elegantly furnished rooms, there is one room in a corner turret that is not used by hotel guests, and that is known as the Ghost Room.

The ghost with her very own room is believed to belong to the late Isabella Shaw, wife of James who built Ballygally Castle. This was a man who built in the baronial style and who demanded of his wife a son and heir. When she failed to provide and produced a daughter instead, John took the baby and locked Isabella in a room in the turret. Isabella, desperate to be reunited with her baby, attempted to escape through a window and fell to her death. The fate of the baby is not known.

Guests are welcome to ascend the stone staircase to experience the Ghost Room for themselves. Most do so without incident, but there was one occasion when a German couple and another

visiting couple with infant in tow asked to see the turret room. They weren't in there for long: 'On entering the "ghost room" our previously smiling gurgling 18-month-old became hysterical with terror. He could not be placated. You have never seen four adults leave a room so quickly!'

Isabella is not the only ghost to have been reported at Ballygally Castle. The spirit of Madam Nixon, who lived at the castle in the 19th century, is said to walk the corridors at night. More often heard than seen, the skirts of her silk dress brush against the walls and she has been known to knock on doors to the confusion of some guests. There was also something that so spooked a guest staying in one of the rooms in the tower beneath the Ghost Room that he ran semi-naked into the hotel's reception. He said he'd been awoken by the sensation of a hand on his back and heard what sounded like a child running about the room. When he was more awake, he remembered he wasn't at home but at a hotel on his own and fled.

Ballygally Castle's conversion into luxury accommodation includes the medieval dungeon, which is available to hire for private dining. One December evening in 2003, the table was laid in readiness for a group of corporate guests. With napkins folded, the glasses polished, chairs tucked in and everything just so, the room was locked up. However, when the manager returned to check the room shortly before the guests' arrival, the table setting had clearly been tampered with. The napkins had been unfolded and those once-gleaming glasses were arranged in a circle and smeared with something undefinable.

Now from the confines of dungeons and turrets to the wilds of County Down.

MOURNE MOUNTAINS, COUNTY DOWN

The Mournes are a granite mountain range in the south-east of the country, the highest in Northern Ireland, and are very accurately designated as an Area of Outstanding Natural Beauty. Beauty they undeniably have in abundance but also tales of ghosts and ghouls, for these mountains, as magnificent as they are, have long been associated with danger and disaster for the traveller who doesn't show due care and respect.

The small seaside town of Newcastle is the natural entry to the Mournes from the north, and has a population of around 8,000 people – and several ghosts. The harbour is said to be haunted by a banshee, who drifts between the moorings. In Irish folklore, the banshee is a female spirit who heralds the death of a family member, usually by shrieking or keening. Overlooking the harbour is Bogey Hill, named after the bogies which were carts used to transport quarried granite. Here a ghostly widow has been seen, looking out to sea and waiting plaintively for a husband who will never return. On 13 January 1843, 14 fishing boats were caught in a storm, of which only two returned. In total 73 men perished, 46 of whom were from Newcastle.

Near Newcastle at the foot of the Mourne Mountains is Tollymore Forest Park, made even more picturesque by the ruined Gothic arches and other garden follies that are the remnants of a stately home. Before it was demolished in the 1950s, Bryansford House played host to American GIs during the war, several of whom saw the spectre of the Blue Lady on the staircase. She is now said to wander the forest, which is even more associated with ghosts since it was used as the location of the Haunted Forest in *Game of Thrones*.

Place names throughout the Mournes are hugely evocative. Take Maggie's Leap, not far from Armour's Hole, a short distance from the Jaws of Hell, after which you come to Bloody Bridge River. These names almost seem to be warnings, suggesting some unhappy fate that befell the unwary who've gone this way before.

Maggie survived, at least in one version of the story, after she leapt the three-metre chasm to escape the advances of some drunken soldiers. Even the eggs she was carrying survived.

At Armour's Hole, however, a father and son got into a drunken quarrel over the son's choice of wife. The father ended up dead at the bottom of the hole, and the son sometime later at the end of a hangman's noose.

The Jaws of Hell got its name following a land dispute, which clearly got well out of hand. When the farmland's tenancy was awarded to people who didn't have local support, those locals rounded up the tenants' cattle, horses and donkeys and drove them all into this chasm and to their deaths.

The Bloody Bridge River, as you may have already guessed, was the scene of a massacre. It happened during the Great Rebellion of 1641, the same uprising that threatened but failed to breach the walls of our previous stop, Ballygally Castle (see page 148). The rebels had prisoners whom they were planning to exchange for some of their own who'd been captured. The exchange was to take place at Downpatrick, but as they approached Newcastle the rebels received word that their comrades had been executed. So they did likewise, spilling blood until the river ran red, their terrible deed immortalised in the name of this place.

Lough Shannagh immortalises a legend, but curiously is not named after the young woman who got lost in the mist and drowned in the lough. It's instead named after the poor animal she was pursuing (it translates as 'Lake of the Fox'). Sheelagh was a highly skilled rider and, as the chieftain's daughter, was permitted to join the men in the hunt. But on one hunt, so intent was she on her quarry that she pursued it into the mist. With visibility low and her riding at full tilt, she and her horse carried on into the lough. Disorientated by the mist, neither Sheelagh nor the horse could see their way back to dry land. Sheelagh's family searched for her for days but to no avail. Her ghost is said to be seen, particularly when mist descends, still flailing in the waters. Some say her distraught father was so consumed with grief that he died soon after. He was buried under trees west of the lough, and now terrifies walkers with his wailing as they pass on the road close by.

CROM, COUNTY FERMANAGH

Travelling westwards from the Mourne Mountains, close to the border with the Republic of Ireland, we come to Crom. This 2,000-acre estate lies on the shores of Upper Lough Erne and is one of Ireland's most important conservation areas, now in the care of the National Trust. Most of the estate comprises riparian woodland – woodland adjacent to a body of water. On land it has one of the country's largest remaining areas of semi-natural oak woodland, containing such biodiversity as to suggest that it dates back to the Neolithic period. The lough is home to one of the UK's biggest populations of otters, and supports a variety of wintering wildfowl, including internationally important numbers of whooper swan. Finally, in the margins, are rare and endangered species, such as Irish lady's-tresses orchids and the fen violet.

While these species struggle to survive elsewhere, here they thrive, indicating a good, healthy ecosystem. Another rare and propitious sighting in these parts is the Lady of the Lake. Famous in Fermanagh folklore – and with a statue and an annual festival in her name in Irvinestown – she would appear in days of old, clad in glowing garments, gliding across the lough and carrying a bunch of beautiful flowers in her hand, a symbol of the natural bounty she heralds.

Many have told tales of a ball of light that appears from time to time hovering over the surface of Upper Lough Erne.

Whether she is Erne, after whom the lough is named and who in Irish mythology was Queen Méabh's lady-in-waiting, is not clear. In that story, Erne and her maidens were fleeing from a giant when they fell into a river and drowned, their bodies dissolving to create Lough Erne. Given the Lady of the Lake comes bearing flowers and the lough's creation story contains a theme common in mythology – that of the divine power of water to give life to the land – the phantom and the myth could be one and the same.

Whether the glowing Lady of the Lake is the same as another phenomenon that has been reported by locals since the early 18th century is also unclear. Many have told tales of a ball of light that appears from time to time, hovering over the surface of Upper Lough Erne. This description is reminiscent of a phenomenon that goes by the name of will-o'-the-wisp (see page 80, Wicken Fen), but these lights are reported hovering over wetlands. Many dismiss such sightings as eruptions of marsh gas, but the lough is too deep and insufficiently stagnant to produce this gas.

Whether the glowing lady and the luminous orb are the same phenomena or different, they evoke no fear. Which can't be said of the experience of an unfortunate couple visiting the lough in 1992, who set out to explore it in a rowboat. Stopping to rest on the island of Inishfendra, the husband stretched out for a nap on a flat rock on the water's edge. Moments later he was wide awake and surrounded by bare-chested men wearing roughly woven trousers with cross-garters below the knee. Grabbing his wife, they powered back to the visitor centre. According to the volunteer to whom they recounted their ordeal, the husband looked completely ashen. The volunteer realised that the spot he had chosen to rest was known to be a votive stone, where pre-Christian Celts would have made offerings to their gods.

Where elements meet, such as here at the water's edge, mysterious things can and do happen, as we shall see at our next destination.

DUNLUCE CASTLE, COUNTY ANTRIM

A nd now to Narnia, or as close to it as we can get without the benefit of a magic wardrobe. When Belfast-born C.S. Lewis was writing *The Chronicles of Narnia*, he looked to the landscape of Ireland, the counties of Ulster in particular. It's said that Dunluce Castle was the inspiration for the royal castle of Cair Paravel. This was the spectacular and enchanted citadel, where it was prophesied that the two Sons of Adam and two Daughters of Eve would assume their thrones, thereby defeating the White Witch. Lewis was clearly possessed of a towering imagination and he would have needed it to give life to this location, as Dunluce Castle has been largely uninhabited since the end of the 17th century. Today, in the care of the Northern Ireland Environment Agency, the shell of Dunluce Castle perches precariously on a basalt outcrop in County Antrim.

However, even in its ruinous state, or perhaps because of it – part of it on land, part of it crumbled into the sea below – it has a liminal quality, that state of being in between two worlds, that invites thoughts of myth and mystery.

The first castle was built on this rocky headland in the 13th century by Richard Óg de Burgh, 2nd Earl of Ulster. Even then it was teetering on the cliff-edge, but the McQuillan family still decided to make it their stronghold from the early 16th century. In those violent and turbulent times, it was necessary for aristocratic families to be able to not only fend off their rivals but also lock up their daughters.

This is what happened to Lord McQuillan when he had arranged a suitor for whom his daughter Maeve didn't much care. Maeve was already in love with another man, far less suitable in her father's eyes, and so she was locked in one of the castle's turrets until she agreed to do her father's bidding. Her love came to her rescue but he chose a wild and stormy night to do it. He broke her free and the two ill-fated lovers clambered into a little rowboat in rough seas to make their escape. They were quickly overwhelmed by the storm and perished in the icy waters. His body was washed ashore but hers was never found. Now, on stormy nights, it's said that Maeve's desolate cries can be heard coming from the north-east tower, as she laments her lost love.

The in-fighting between clans continued unabated and towards the end of the 16th century it was the McQuillans versus the MacDonnells, led by Sorley Boy MacDonnell. These two families had tussled over Dunluce for decades until the Battle of Aura. Exemplifying the power of a good story, there are two accounts of this battle – the traditional and the historical. The traditional dates the battle to 1559 and describes how the night before, the canny MacDonnells cut and spread rushes over the boggy terrain; the following day the McQuillans charged blindly into the bog where the MacDonnell men made quick work of them. The historical account is dated to 1583 and describes how the McQuillans, who'd gained reinforcements from the O'Neill clan together with two companies of English musketeers, were simply ill-suited to the marshy terrain with their cavalry and heavy infantry when compared with the relatively small force assembled by Sorley Boy MacDonnell.

Sorley Boy, whichever version you believe, had won the day but had also unfortunately drawn the attention of Queen Elizabeth. The MacDonnells were now simply too powerful and had to be put in their place. In 1584 Elizabeth instructed her Lord Deputy of Ireland, Sir John Perrot, to crush Dunluce. Accounts of Sir John Perrot suggest he would have enjoyed his work: thought by some to be an illegitimate son of Henry VIII, whom he resembled, as a young man he was described as having 'a violent and arbitrary disposition' and being 'much addicted to brawling'. After two days of military bombardment, Sorley Boy surrendered Dunluce Castle and Sir John installed Peter Carey as constable of the castle.

Several people have reported feeling a chill on entering this tower, as if a presence without body or warmth has pushed past them.

Sorley Boy sought to appease and negotiate with the English government and eventually, having sworn his allegiance, Queen Elizabeth deigned in 1586 to restore Dunluce Castle to him. His first act on regaining the keys to his castle was to have Peter Carey hanged from the ramparts of the south-east tower. It's said that Carey's ghost – and you'll know it's him by the ponytail and purple cloak that he sports – has wandered the tower ever since. Several people have reported feeling a chill on entering this tower, as if a presence without body or warmth has pushed past them.

Now we push on and across the water to Rathlin Island, small but with a mythological footprint.

RATHLIN ISLAND, COUNTY ANTRIM

Rathlin Island lies just six miles off County Antrim's north coast and 16 miles from the southern tip of the Mull of Kintyre. As such, it has long been used as a strategic stopping-off point between Northern Ireland and Scotland by travellers both mythological and historical.

The island is part of the Causeway Coast, and perhaps the most famous story from these parts is that of Finn McCool, the giant who built the Giant's Causeway in order to do battle with his Scottish rival, Benandonner. Local tradition says that Finn's wife, Oona, was helping her husband build the causeway and

went to Scotland to get more rocks, but dropped a pile from her apron into the sea on the way home, creating Rathlin Island.

While Rathlin Island is clearly a formation belonging to the coast of Northern Ireland, *its* most famous story involves one of the most celebrated Scotsmen of all time, Robert the Bruce. Robert I was King of Scots from 1306 to his death in 1329 and led his country during the First War of Scottish Independence against England. Shortly after Robert's coronation, the King of England, Edward I, moved against him and defeated the Scottish forces at the Battle of Methven, forcing them to flee. They sought refuge on Rathlin Island, in its castle which at the time was owned by a Scoto-Irish family. It was here, according to legend, that Robert witnessed a spider trying to weave its web, repeatedly failing but refusing to give up. When the spider had failed for the sixth time, Robert decided that if the spider succeeded on the seventh attempt, he would return to Scotland and take up arms once more. The spider did indeed succeed, as did Robert the Bruce, at the Battle of Bannockburn, although it took him another eight years. It makes a fine and inspirational tale, but Rathlin Island has witnessed far darker episodes that lead many to think it's haunted and home to the Devil himself.

What was at times a place of sanctuary, at others was a scene of unspeakable brutality and violence. In the 16th century, the English being heartily sick of the continued and combined resistance of the Scottish and Irish, Queen Elizabeth instructed her favourite pirate, Francis Drake, to attack Rathlin Island, which was being used as a base by the MacDonnells. Under the leadership of Sorley Boy MacDonnell (see page 156, Dunluce Castle), the MacDonnells thought to keep their wives and children, the sick and elderly on the island for safekeeping, while they waged their military campaigns on the mainland. This made it an irresistible target for the English who, on 25 July 1575, launched their offensive on the island and its castle until the MacDonnells surrendered. Despite the surrender, the English killed everyone on Rathlin, while Drake ensured no reinforcements could come from Scotland. In all, it's thought more than 600 Scots and Irish –men, women and children – were killed.

A century later the MacDonnells were again under attack, but this time from Scottish enemies, the Campbells. In 1642, Sir Duncan Campbell ordered his men to kill all Catholic MacDonnells living on the island. It's said that around 300 MacDonnells were murdered while their wives and children looked on from Crocascreedlin. Then the witnesses were marched to the highest cliff and driven over onto the rocks below. Legend has it that for centuries after the slaughter, their screams could be heard echoing from their viewpoint, which translates as 'Hill of the Screaming'.

When the fourth cup was full, the spectral hand took it and withdrew into the shadows once more. They say the hand belonged to the Devil himself.

These are not Rathlin's only ghosts; with so much slaughter on the island, local stories of hauntings are rife. One of the better-known tales tells of how three fishermen were taking a break in a cave on the west of the island. After lighting a fire so they could boil water to make tea, they placed their cups on a large, flat boulder. As the tea was being poured, a hand emerged from the shadows and placed a fourth cup on the boulder. Gripped with terror, the fishermen didn't dare to turn to look at their mysterious visitor, but continued to pour the tea. When the fourth cup was full, the spectral hand took it and withdrew into the shadows once more. They say the hand belonged to the Devil himself.

Having travelled to the northernmost tip of Northern Ireland, it's across the North Channel we next go to the west coast of Scotland.

SCOTLAND

CULZEAN CASTLE, SOUTH AYRSHIRE

High atop a cliff, commanding the finest views over the Firth of Clyde and looking resplendent in all directions, is Culzean Castle. Pronounced 'cull-ane', this castle is the 18th-century masterpiece of Robert Adam. While Adam is perhaps best known as a Neo-classical architect, a style that he elevated to stunning effect on country houses and public buildings all over Scotland and England, Culzean is regarded as the epitome of the Picturesque movement in Scotland, combining informal architectural flourishes with regularly ordered classical features.

For all its confident beauty, it might be difficult to imagine this castle as the purgatorial haunt of several sad souls – at least seven at the last count and investigations are ongoing. In September 2023, the *Ayr Advertiser* ran a story about a group of enthusiasts in the paranormal who visited Culzean and captured on camera several incidents, providing evidence of significant activity at the castle. A recurring manifestation was the disembodied voice of a man with a thick Scottish accent, which apparently followed the group both inside the castle and in the caves beneath.

The most famous and the most often reported ghost – because presumably it's hard to keep a low profile with this occupation – is the bagpiper. The story goes that he was sent together with his dog into the caves to prove to locals that they weren't haunted. To stir up anything that might be lurking in the shadows, he started piping as he made his way inside, his dog close behind. After a while the piping faded and only the dog's occasional bark could be heard. Then, all went quiet. A party went in search of them but no trace could be found. Ever since and every so often, the sound of pipes rises unbidden up from the caves and through the castle, and the figure of a piper is seen in a spot near the castle known as Piper's Brae.

Inside the castle there have been sightings of numerous apparitions, but there are few stories to go with them and their identities have remained as mysterious as their appearances. We do, however, know that two of the castle's spectres are women – one who is seen wearing a ball gown and another who is known as the White Lady, thought to be a mistreated servant. Below stairs, along the corridors close to the kitchen the ghost of a girl is sometimes seen running. Even further below, in the castle dungeons, is the scene of something so gruesome, so traumatic, that its shockwaves continue to be felt.

This story dates to a time before Adam's castle was built, when the struggle for lands between clans was that bit more brutish and lawless. In 1570, Earl Gilbert, chief of Clan Kennedy, had his eyes on Crossraguel Abbey in nearby Maybole. He decided the most effective course of action was to abduct the cleric who had the power to sign over the deeds and take him to the Black Vault, which was located under the future site of Culzean Castle (or possibly nearby Dunure Castle, according to some sources). Gilbert Kennedy had the cleric carried by his baker, his cook and his pantryman into the vault, where he was stripped naked and bound to a spit and then roasted over a great fire. Close to death, the cleric agreed to sign over the deeds. Six days later he was roasted again so he would sign a confirmation document. Somehow the poor man survived this terrible ordeal. For this abhorrent act, Gilbert Kennedy was fined £2,000 by the Privy Council and forced to pay the cleric a pension for life. He kept the land, however, and the cleric spent the rest of his life in terrible pain. Since that time, usually on a Sunday morning, it's said that the crackle and roar of a great fire can sometimes be heard coming from the depths of the castle vaults, accompanied by screams of pain and cries for mercy.

GLENCOE, HIGHLAND

As the screams emanating from the dungeons of our previous destination fade from our imagination, we make our way north to Glencoe, where the ghostly cries heard on the anniversary of one of the bloodiest events in Scottish history would make whispers of what's heard at Culzean.

The two clans involved in the events of 13 February 1692 were the MacDonalds and the Campbells; it's true they had a long history of feuding, but it was the political plotting and scheming of William III's government that brought matters to such bloodshed. The Jacobite risings (of which more later) had begun a few years earlier and saw Highland clans pitted against each other: those that supported the deposed King James (the Latin for 'James' is *Jacobus*, hence the name) and those that pledged allegiance to William III. The MacDonalds were Jacobites, but after William threatened to punish in the severest way any clan that refused to sign an oath of allegiance before 1 January, the chief of the MacDonalds, MacIain, decided it was safer to accede. He was a few days past the deadline, but he believed he had done enough to keep his clan safe. Sadly, their fate had already been sealed, the government being only too glad for an excuse to kill off a few more Highlanders.

For nearly two weeks from the end of January, 120 government redcoats under the command of a Campbell clansman had been staying with the MacDonalds at Glencoe. On 13 February the order was given: 'You are hereby ordered to fall upon the Rebells, the McDonalds of Glenco, and putt all to the sword under Seventy.' MacIain was the first to be killed and, in all, it's believed 38 men, women and children were slaughtered in the attack, with many more succumbing to the cold having fled into the open countryside.

The scale of the treachery, as much as the number of innocent people killed, has made this massacre especially notorious and has reverberated down through history. As majestic as the scenery of Glencoe is, in mid-February it really does feel like the most desolate and, in the knowledge of its history, profoundly sad place. That the cries of the fallen still echo in the mountains is really hardly surprising.

In a curious and somewhat spooky footnote, there is the tale of a local witch called Corrag. It's said she foresaw the massacre and tried to warn the MacDonalds, but they ignored her. She took herself off into the mountains, wrapped up warmly, until it was safe to return. Seeing the awful reality of her prediction, she went into MacIain's empty house, took his broadsword and threw it into Loch Leven, saying: 'So long as this sword lays undisturbed by man, no man from this Glen will die by the sword again.'

A local historian who was familiar with this story was curious enough to investigate whether it was just a fairy tale. Sure enough, when he checked the records, despite the MacDonalds being at the Battle of Culloden (see page 168), not one was killed. Then he checked all the major battles in which Scotsmen were engaged – Waterloo, Trafalgar, Balaclava – and again, no sons of Glencoe were in the recorded deaths, even in the first two years of the First World War when casualties ran into millions. Then, on 1 July 1916, came one of the bloodiest battles of all time, the Battle of the Somme, in which nearly 20,000 British soldiers were killed on that first day alone. Seven men from Glencoe were killed in that battle, the first to die in conflict since 1692.

Here's the sad twist to this tale: in June 1916, a dredger had been at work deepening Loch Leven to improve passage for large ships and in the process had brought up an ancient artefact. On the evening of 30 June the captain of the dredger took his find to the pub, proudly brandishing an old sword and explaining where it had come from. This drew a horrified reaction from locals who knew the story of Corrag; they grabbed the sword from the perplexed captain and threw it back into the loch, hoping they were in time. Sadly, it seems they were not.

BOLESKINE HOUSE, HIGHLAND

Continuing north and stopping short of Inverness by approximately 20 miles and about half-way up the south-east bank of Loch Ness you come to Boleskine House (pronounced 'boll-es-kin'). This property gained notoriety when it was sought out and bought by one Aleister Crowley, apparently for twice its market value at the time, so intent was he on acquiring it.

Aleister Crowley has been described as many things, but most commonly as an occultist, philosopher, magician, writer, poet, painter and, finally, mountaineer. The rugged beauty of the Trossachs National Park would most certainly have appealed to Crowley's artistic side, but it was specifically for the practice of

the darker arts that he wanted to buy Boleskine. However, long before Crowley came to the area – or perhaps forming part of its attraction – it had come to be associated with strange and terrible events.

The house, a single-storey hunting lodge, was built in the 1760s by Colonel Archibald Fraser of Clan Fraser of Lovat, whose relative Lord Lovat had been beheaded for high treason in 1747. The site chosen by the colonel for his lodge was formerly occupied by a kirk that had burned down with the entire congregation trapped inside. But even before that there were grisly goings-on, as recorded in parish archives from the 17th century. Minister Thomas Houston, whose likeness is carved into a headstone in the graveyard, was reportedly called upon by his parishioners to deal with the animated corpses that were roaming the graveyard, having been raised from the dead by a local wizard named An Cruinair Friseal.

Such was the dark history of Boleskine House when Crowley bought it, but there were more specific reasons for his purchase. He had obtained a translation of *The Book of the Sacred Magic of Abramelin the Mage* by Samuel Liddell MacGregor Mathers, fellow occultist and founder of the Hermetic Order of the Golden Dawn. In the book, prefaced with dire warnings to never attempt the ritual, were instructions on how to invoke one's Guardian Angel. If that sounds like something that might actually be quite a useful thing to do, the caveat it comes with is the necessary first step of summoning the Twelve Kings and Dukes of Hell. Once called forth, they must be vanquished so that the summoner can be freed from their negative influence, thereby gaining access to his Guardian Angel, who in turn would grant the mage (magician) the ability to control the demons who run the universe, raise the dead, heal the sick, find great treasures and fly. Crowley thought this was worth the risk, ignored the warnings and started making the necessary preparations.

First, and always tremendously important, was location. As stated in his book *The Confessions of Aleister Crowley*, 'the first essential is a house in a more or less secluded situation. There should be a door opening to the north from the room of which you make your oratory. Outside this door, you construct a terrace covered with fine river sand. This ends in a "lodge" where the spirits may congregate'.

At the time Crowley had rooms on Chancery Lane in London – so, far from remote – in which he had a black room where he kept a human skeleton that he would feed with blood and the remains of small animals. (According to Crowley: 'The idea was to give it life, but I never got further than causing the bones to become covered with a viscous slime ....') Crowley needed to do better and Boleskine House was deemed the perfect place to set up operations.

Here, in 1899, Crowley began the lengthy preparations, which should be expected to take at least six months. However, he got called away by the Hermetic Order of the Golden Dawn on occult business before he'd had time to fully banish the demons that had been summoned – some reports say 115 had been summoned rather than the intended 12. We've all had that nagging 'did I leave the cooker on?' feeling, but very few of us have had the 'did I leave the portal to hell open?' equivalent. The site where Boleskine House stood (it was all but destroyed by fires in 2015 and 2019) had already seen some terrible things, but it was about to get worse.

Doors would spontaneously spring open and slam shut, when all was calm outside.

A darkness gathered and clung to the place, strange figures were seen in the area and locals went far out of their way to avoid the house. Crowley wrote: 'While I was preparing the talismans, squares of vellum inscribed in Indian ink, a task which I undertook in the sunniest room in the house, I had to use an artificial light even on the brightest days. It was a darkness which might almost be felt. The lode and terrace, moreover, soon became peopled with shadowy shapes, sufficiently substantial, as a rule, to be almost opaque.'

The darkness spread to the people connected most closely to the house – although Crowley seems to have been spared. The lodge keeper, a teetotaller for 20 years, went on a three-day drinking binge and tried to kill his wife and children. Even worse befell the housekeeper, Hugh Gillies, when two of his children died suddenly and unexpectedly. Crowley spent less and less time at the property and finally left in 1913.

Amazingly, Boleskine's reputation didn't deter others from making it their home. Some apparently lived here unvisited by tragedy, but we do know that in 1965 a retired major took his own life in what was Crowley's bedroom (his housekeeper had a premonition seven days before the awful event when she heard a shotgun fire inside but found the house empty).

Then in 1970 Boleskine was bought by another hell-raiser, but of the more metaphorical rock-and-roll variety rather than the literal necromancing kind. Jimmy Page, guitarist and founder of the rock band Led Zeppelin, had been fascinated by Crowley from a young age and was a collector of Crowley memorabilia. When the opportunity came up to buy the house where Crowley had once lived and performed his rituals, Page thought it would make a great atmosphere in which to write songs. He also used it as a location for a fantasy sequence that featured in the 1976 film *The Song Remains the Same*, which was filmed at night on the mountainside directly behind Boleskine House.

Though buying it was the fulfilment of an ambition, Page said the house gave off 'bad vibes' in an interview with *Rolling Stone* magazine in 1975. He went on to say, 'When I go there with friends – writers and other creative people – I find that it crystallises things for them in a very short time. Of course, it causes a lot of upheaval for some people as well.'

Page didn't experience too much of this himself – he spent relatively little time at Boleskine – but his friend Malcolm Dent, who moved in to oversee renovations, recounted many inexplicable and unsettling occurrences. One night, described by him as the most terrifying of his life, he awoke to what sounded like a wild animal snorting outside his bedroom door. When he summoned up the courage to open the door, he saw nothing but said 'whatever was there was very, very evil and I was very, very frightened'. Another friend who spent the night at Boleskine claimed to have been attacked by 'some kind of devil'. It was claimed doors would spontaneously spring open and slam shut, when all was calm outside, and furniture and rugs would be moved around and piled up.

Page sold Boleskine in 1992 and there seem to have been happier spells of ownership, first when it was converted and run as a hotel and later lived in as a holiday home. Then in 2015 a fire broke out, which was believed to have started in the kitchen, and gutted the interior. Fortunately, as there was no one in the house at the time, there were no casualties.

In 2019, the ruins of Boleskine House and 22 acres of land were put on the market and bought by the Boleskine House Foundation, a charitable organisation. Its aim was to restore the house to its origins as a Jacobean and Georgian hunting lodge, and to preserve house and estate together as a historic landmark and valuable piece of Scottish heritage. The foundation's task was not helped by another fire, a suspected arson attack shortly after acquisition. While Boleskine's association with Crowley and the occult is not something the foundation emphasises, you can purchase an Abramelin candle from their website, the recipe for the incense being described in *The Book of the Sacred Magic of Abramelin the Mage*. It goes without saying, do not leave burning candles unattended and be sure to banish all demons before leaving the house.

CULLODEN BATTLEFIELD, HIGHLAND

The number of lost souls at Boleskine House are as nothing compared to the number who fell at Culloden Moor, a short distance north-east from our previous paranormal pitstop. This is the site of the last pitched battle fought on British soil. It was over quickly – it's thought to have lasted under an hour – but it was extremely bloody. The last battle it may have been, but some say ghosts of the combatants fight on to this day. On the anniversary of this bloodshed that turned the tide – mostly red – of Highland history, it's said that the fallen soldiers rise again, the sounds of their anguished cries and clashing swords filling the air.

Here, on 16 April 1746, the last of the Jacobite risings ran its course and Culloden Moor ran with the blood of around 1,300 soldiers, 1,250 of them Jacobites. The first of the risings was in 1689, after the deposition of James VII of Scotland and James II of England and Ireland in the Glorious Revolution of the previous year and the subsequent attempt to restore him to the throne. The Jacobites had a stronghold in the Highlands, so this was always going to be where their final act of resistance took place.

In 1744 Charles Edward Stuart, the grandson of the ousted King James and better known as Bonnie Prince Charlie, made his way through France to drum up additional anti-English support, landing on the west coast of Scotland in 1745 and triggering the final Jacobite rising. The Jacobites, having gained more support from the Highland chieftains, made early gains, capturing Carlisle, marching through Lancaster, Preston and Manchester, and advancing as far as Derby by the end of the year. But government troops rallied and the support promised by the French and by English Jacobites failed to materialise. Bonnie Prince Charlie decided they needed to regroup and ordered the retreat back into Scotland. Funds and morale were running low, and there were many deserters. By the time of the final encounter at Culloden Moor, it's estimated that the Jacobites were outnumbered 9,000 to 5,000. This combined with the superior artillery of the government troops and the boggy ground of the moor, which hampered the usually highly effective Highland charge, meant it was all over very quickly for the Jacobites.

Visitors to Culloden Moor can sense its desolation, and many have reported seeing and hearing the ghosts of the fallen.

For his role in the Battle of Culloden, the Duke of Cumberland, the youngest son of George II, gained the epithet 'Butcher' Cumberland. It was on his orders that every survivor of the battle be rounded up and killed. He went further still with his reprisals on the Highlanders who assisted Bonnie Prince Charlie. The Scottish clan system was treated with ruthless hostility and Cumberland set about dismantling Highland culture by disarming the clans, banning the wearing of Highland dress, and suppressing the use of certain surnames and the Gaelic language. There are reports of government troops burning down farms, homesteads and villages, and driving women and children from their homes.

Such is the tragic and much-mourned legacy of Culloden. What transpired here was more than a slaughter, approaching a form of ethnic cleansing. Visitors to Culloden Moor can sense its desolation, and many have reported seeing and hearing the ghosts of the fallen, in particular the ghost of a tall man in full Highland dress, looking utterly despairing and muttering the word 'Defeated' over and over. Tartan features in other accounts too, seen draped over the ground where so many fell. In 1936, a woman reported lifting a tartan cloth that was lying on one of the grave mounds to reveal an apparition of a severely wounded Highlander.

Diana Gabaldon, author of the *Outlander* series, references Culloden in her historical fantasy novels and has visited the battlefield for her research. In an interview, broadcast on the Gaelic-language BBC Alba channel, Diana maintained that she doesn't possess any special psychic abilities but that she very much sensed the spirits at Culloden, adding that anyone who visits the site would experience the same. She said: 'I've walked a lot of battlefields. Most are not haunted – that one is. Without being metaphysical at all, I can feel all the people there. I can't talk about them or I'll cry.'

CRATHES CASTLE, ABERDEENSHIRE

Crathes is another fairy-tale castle, which Scotland has in such profusion, but dig a little deeper and there lurks a more sinister story.

As we return to the gentility of the castle-dwelling aristocracy of Scotland, the ghosts in this castle would testify that while the owners might have possessed wealth and refinement, they were no less murderous for it. Just think of Lord and Lady Macbeth in Shakespeare's story of ambition gone bad, and you can imagine the skulduggery required to establish your place in society and the lengths you had to go to in order to keep it.

Until it was given to the National Trust for Scotland in 1951, from the time of its construction in the mid-16th century Crathes Castle served as the ancestral home of the Burnett of Leys family. Before then they had lived in a wooden fortress on an artificial island in the middle of a bog. While the land was a gift from Robert the Bruce, it seems the family had to work hard to attain their status as lairds and ladies of a castle.

Inside this beautiful pink-rendered tower house, along with the rich furnishings, ornamented ceilings and fine family portraits, are said to be the ghosts of two women, one thought to be a laird's daughter and the other a would-be lady. The more famous of the two is known as the Green Lady, made more so by the fact that one of the people who reported seeing her was Queen Victoria. She described a green mist floating across the room before it scooped up an infant and disappeared into the fireplace. Others have seen the spirit of a young woman in a green dress cradling a baby by the fireplace, and some have seen a green orb travelling across the room.

There is a theory that the baby was the result of an affair with a stable boy, and both mother and child were killed to save the family's reputation. In the 1800s, during a renovation, the bones of a child were discovered under the hearth of the fireplace, so it cannot be denied that a child's death was covered up.

The second, lesser-known, ghost is called the White Lady. She is believed to be the spirit of a young woman who was in love with the son of Laird Alexander and Lady Agnes Burnett. We are fortunate that her story is included in *Legends of Leys; Oral Traditions of the Burnett Family* (1856).

In the 1500s, and a long time after, if you were a member of the Scottish gentry you didn't have the luxury of marrying for love. Laird Alexander died when his son (also Alexander) was only six years old, so the responsibility of preserving the family's status fell to his widow, something she guarded most zealously. So when young Alexander, aged 17 and already betrothed to the daughter of a duke, declared his love for Bertha de Bernard, Lady Agnes wasn't having it.

Bertha was a visiting cousin from France, which was embroiled in the Anglo-French War, and so she stayed at the Burnetts' island home for some months. After Alexander had announced his intention to marry Bertha, he had to go away for a time to deal with a land dispute. This gave Lady Agnes ample opportunity to act. Bertha became gravely ill with some sort of wasting disease and by the time Alexander returned she was dead. He found her laid out on a bier in the great hall and, overcome with emotion, he began to feel faint. He reached out for a cup of wine that was standing on a table nearby, but before he could drink from it his mother dashed it out of his hand.

As if that wasn't damning enough, a year after Bertha's death came final proof. While the family were having supper in the hall, Bertha's father, who had heard of his daughter's death on his way over from France, stormed into the room and angrily accused Lady Agnes. In a scene fit for *Macbeth*, a chill gripped the room and wall hangings began moving as if by some sudden wind. Lady Agnes sat bolt upright, transfixed by something unseen and began screaming, 'She comes! She comes!' before dropping down dead.

In time, Alexander went on to marry Janet Hamilton and, deciding to leave his heartbreak behind in the island fortress, he had Crathes Castle built a little distance away. It's said that once a year, on the anniversary of Bertha's death, the White Lady makes her way from the site of the old island home to the beautiful castle built by her lover.

MARY KING'S CLOSE, EDINBURGH

From fairy-tale castles to inner-city squalor – a place where it's easy to imagine how the poorest members of Scottish society once lived. Today, Mary King's Close is a major tourist attraction, a preserved 17th-century warren of streets beneath Edinburgh's Royal Mile. One of the sources of fascination for visitors is the close's reputation for paranormal activity, which is saying something in a city that is thought to be one of the most haunted in the world. Murderers and body-snatchers make up just a part, but a very compelling one, of the city's folklore. However, those stories might even be considered glamorous next to the grim tales of life, and death, in Mary King's Close.

In the Middle Ages, this part of the city had become one of its most densely populated areas. Edinburgh's housing solution was to build tenements, which rose seven or so storeys high. Down on the lower levels, in permanent damp gloom, choked by a thousand cooking fires and awash with the effluent of its residents, streets like this were always going to be a breeding ground for disease. And medieval disease was unimaginably dreadful and devastating. The Great Plague of 1645 left over 15,000 of Edinburgh's citizens dead, around half the city's population. The residents of the rat-infested Mary King's Close didn't stand a chance.

This outbreak was, mercifully, the city's last. By the end of the century, pressure on housing in the city had started to build again and people returned to the close. As soon as they did, the sightings of the spirits of plague victims began. Thomas Coltheart and his wife moved to the close in 1685 and they were beset by apparitions: a man's disembodied head, a severed arm, a grizzled ghost dog, a phantom child.

Life continued in the close, with occasional visitations from the dead, until the construction of the Royal Exchange, now Edinburgh City Chambers, in the mid-18th century. It was built partially on top of the close, causing part of it to be demolished, part of it to be buried. Some residents refused or could not afford to leave their subterranean dwellings, but eventually the last resident moved out in 1902, the close was sealed off to the public and for decades forgotten about. Almost.

The Real Mary King's Close opened as a visitor attraction in 2003, but there were unofficial tours of this secret place, known only to locals and spoken about in hushed tones, from the 1980s. Its grisly history and ghostly reputation drew curious individuals, determined to catch sight of one of the many spirits believed to dwell here. One of them has been named as Andrew Chesney, whose ghost is seen as a short, elderly man with a worried look on his face. Another ghost is believed to be that of Mary King, a tall woman in a black dress, after whom the close is named. Then there's a nameless child, who makes scratching noises inside the chimney in which they died as they swept. Some claim to have had their hands scratched when they reached inside the chimney. But the most famous ghost of all is Annie.

In 1992 a Japanese medium, Aiko Gibo, came to Mary King's Close with a documentary film crew. On arriving in one room, Gibo was overcome by feelings of sickness, hunger, cold and sadness. Initially refusing to enter, she did so after apparently being invited in by the ghost of a little girl who tugged at her hand. Gibo was able to determine that the girl's name was Annie and she was a plague victim. The girl told Gibo that she'd been abandoned by her family and that she'd lost her doll. Gibo ended their interaction with the gift of a doll and, since then, this ghost has been known as Abandoned Annie and the room in which she resides is piled high with dolls left by visitors.

INDEX

Henry VIII 32, 35, 36,
44–5, 85–6, 104–5,
106, 158
Hermetic Order of the
Golden Dawn 171, 172
hexes 78
see also curses
High Peak Estate,
Derbyshire 68–72
Highland
Boleskine House
169–74, 175
Culloden Battlefield
175–7
Glencoe 167–9
highwaymen 30
hill forts, Iron Age 66
Hinton Ampner,
Hampshire 46–8
Hobart, Sir Henry, 1st
Baronet 87
Hobart, Sir Henry, 4th
Baronet 87–9
Hoggard, Brian 136
Holmes, Sherlock 18
Holy Grail 25
Holy Trinity Church,
Buckfastleigh 18
horseback, ghosts on 29
headless horsemen
16, 87
horses, phantom 109
headless 87
hotels 57
Ballygally Castle
148–50
Boleskine House 174
George and Pilgrims
Hotel 26
Lumley Castle 129–30
House of Commons 58
House of Lords 58
houses
Blickling Hall 36, 44,
85–9, 105
Boleskine House
169–74, 175
Coughton Court 57–9
Gunby 73–4

Hinton Ampner 46–8
Llanerchaeron 138–41
Lyme 94–6
magical protection
for 136
Newton House 135–8
Nunnington Hall
104–6
Plas Newydd 141–3
Raynham Hall 83–5
Samlesbury Hall 96–8,
101
Seaton Delaval Hall
122, 123–5
Treasurer's House
106–9
see also manor houses;
summer houses
Houses of Parliament 37
see also House of
Commons; House
of Lords
Houston, Thomas 170
Howard, Catherine 44,
45, 105
Huguenots 33
human remains, discovery
21–4, 29, 30, 36, 43, 48,
69, 70, 96, 121, 179
human sacrifice 29, 66
Humphries, John 28,
29, 30
Hundred Years' War
39, 94
Hyatt, Sophie 76–8

incubi 30
India cricket team 130
Inishfendra 155
Ipswich Museum 90
Ireland 141
Iron Age 38, 66
Irvinestown 154

Jackson's Oxford Journal
49–51
Jacobean era 85, 135, 174
Jacobite risings 167,
175–7

Jamaica 46, 80
James VI and I 36–7, 58
James VII and II 167, 175
Jenkes, Rowland 52
Jervis, Admiral 48
jewels 15, 24, 38
Jones, John 140
Joseph of Arimathea 25
Jutes 38

Keary, Annie, *Mia and
Charlie* 106
Kendal Mercury, The
(newspaper) 103
Kennedy, Gilbert 166
Kent
Canterbury Cathedral
38–40
Kingdom of 38
Kineton 55
King, Mary 182
King's Dragoons 80
Kitts Steps 20

Ladies of Llangollen
141–3
Lady of the Lake 154–5
Lady's Grave 95
Ladywood 79–80
lakes 6, 14, 88, 95, 102–3,
111, 168, 169
Lancashire
Pendle Hill 99–102
Samlesbury Hall 96–8,
101
Langton-Massingberd,
Emily 74
Lantern Man 81–2
Law, John 100
Le Neve, Oliver 87–8
Led Zeppelin 173
Lee, Brett 130
Leeds General Infirmary
114
Leeds Union Workhouse
112
Leeds University Medical
School 113
Legh, Joan 94